THE

WHOLESOME

TRUTH

ABOUT

HEALING

THE WHOLESOME TRUTH ABOUT HEALING

Yomi Akinpelu

PNEUMA SPRINGS PUBLISHING UK

Unless otherwise indicated, all Scripture quotations are taken from the King James Version of the Holy Bible.

Scriptures noted AMP are taken from the Amplified Bible.

Scriptures noted NKJV are taken from the New King James Version.

Scriptures noted NASB are taken from the New American Standard Bible.

Scriptures noted NIV are taken from the New International Version of the Bible.

Scriptures noted TLB are taken from The Living Bible.

The Wholesome Truth About Healing

Copyright © 2006 Yomi Akinpelu

ISBN10: 0-9545510-7-9
ISBN13: 978-0-954551-07-0

First Published 2006 by Pneuma Springs Publishing

Cover design, editing and typesetting by:
Pneuma Springs Publishing
A Subsidiary of Pneuma Springs Ltd.
230 Lower Road, Belvedere Kent, DA17 6DE.
E: admin@pneumasprings.co.uk
W: www.pneumasprings.co.uk

A catalogue record for this book is available from the British Library.

"From the cowardice that shrinks from new truth,
From the laziness that is content with half-truths,
From the arrogance that thinks it knows all truth,
O God of Truth, deliver us"
ANCIENT PRAYER

DEDICATIONS

To Jehovah Rapha my Healer and family Physician.
To my children – Joshua and Gloria;
Through whom God is faithfully teaching me that healing is the children's bread.
To those precious people looking to God for healing; this is the acceptable year of the Lord.
And to all the co-labourers with Christ in His healing ministry.

ACKNOWLEDGEMENTS

Special Thanks

To my husband for his generosity, his full support, for believing in me and encouraging me to pursue my dreams. Also for his superb editorial contribution to this book, and his penchant for excellence.

To my Mother & Father whose subtle influence continues to encourage me to be the best.

To my Pastors; Pastor Albert & Sister Bose, Pastor Jonathan, Pastor Ola-Vincent, Pastor Nathan, Pastor Timothy, Pastor Philip, Rev. Abbih & Minister David. Thank you for your prayers and anointed   teaching.

To my prayer partners and friends; Abi Onaderu, Bunmi Mabo & Titi Ayodele, keep the 'paga' going, the best is yet to come.

To my sisters, Funmilola Aina and Funmilayo Adepegba for their generosity and unconditional love.

To Pastor Ode & Kemi Eyeoyibo for their encouragement and all the books (still on loan)

To my friends for their encouragement when I wrote my first book: **"A Matter of Life & Death"**. I must mention a few;   Mr. Toyin Oyin-Adeniji, Bayo & Agatha Ademiju, Pastor Yomi & Banke Olowoyo, Bayo Emmanuel, Uncle Victor Ovieghara, Minister Paul Babalogbon, Yinka Adeduntan, Dr Sola Mabo, Yinka Oyesiku, Wale Ipefuran, Kenny & Morenike Ajayi, Yolande Grace Nziou & Temitope Alebiosu.

Tackling the tough questions
Did miracles pass away with the apostolic age?
Does God desire perfect health for all his children?
Why are some healed and others not?

CONTENTS

FOREWORD

Yomi is emerging as an outstanding Christian writer of our time. She constantly addresses the challenges this generation faces. Her aptness to teach and strong bible base clearly feed her books and give them balance, practical relevance and spiritual depth. 'The Wholesome Truth About Healing' is another excellent writ. Does God still heal today? Did healing go out with the apostles of the Lamb? Is healing sporadic and unpredictable? This book brings clarity to these pertinent questions - just like Jesus answered the leper when he questioned his willingness to heal;

> Mathew 8:2-3 'And behold, a leper came and worshiped Him, saying, Lord, if You are willing, You can make me clean. Then Jesus put out His hand and touched him, saying, I am willing; be cleansed. Immediately his leprosy was cleansed.

The mix between theological arguments and spiritual truth is striking. This book is not the typical, sometimes shallow Pentecostal exposé but provides historical, biblical and practical perspectives that leave the title of the book fair and representative. 'The Wholesome Truth about Healing' is worth every page it is written on, and comes highly recommend to every Christian.

God is the Healer, and the blood covenant of Jesus makes provision for healing. Cancer, terminal disease, HIV and all twenty first century physical and mental maladies must yield to His ultimate authority. He is a miracle worker and this book points to His true Person, love and mercy. It gives practical tips on how to receive healing and maintain good health. I am sure you will be blessed as you read.

Dr Albert Odulele
Senior Pastor
Glory House Churches, International

Chapter 1

Opening Thoughts
Where is the power that truly changes lives?

The room resembled a scene from an overcrowded London train during the rush hour. People were packed side to side like sardines in a tin. There was no more room in the house, still the crowd pressed closer to hear His words because He taught with such authority. Suddenly the roof above flew open, and down came a quilt, upon which lay a paralysed man. The crowd watched with bated breath. What kind of conviction made these men raise the roof just to get their sick friend into the presence of the Teacher. Jesus saw faith in the daring act of these men, and said to the paralytic, your sins are forgiven, stand up, take up your quilt and go home. The man stood up at once, squeezed through the crowd and went on his way, glorifying God, he even had a spring in his steps. The crowd went wild with amazement and glorified God, they had never seen anything quite like this before! (Mark 2:1-12, Luke 5:17-26).

Christianity is more than mere doctrine; it is power. It is power to transform our lives, power to destroy the evil that prevents us from loving God and our neighbour. Jesus came to bring us a new life, a share in God's own life. We claim to believe these things, but where is the reality of it? Where is the power that truly changes lives? Is the gospel just a talking game about bygone days and the life after, or does Jesus aid a desperate person who needs help here and now? I believe that the ministry of healing is what lifts the central doctrine of redemption from the realm of the abstract into the reality of men's lives. My own experiences and understanding of God's word leads me to the conclusion that healing is the most convincing demonstration to most people, that God is with us, that he is not "out there" beyond the reach of human compassion, but is a very present help in times of trouble.

This book represents years of thoughtful reflection, research, prayer, study and experience. As you read, you will become a partaker of the deepest convictions and innermost deliberations of the author. This book will challenge your thinking, inspire you, and build your confidence in God's willingness to heal. It will give you a wholesome understanding of healing, by providing you with answers to many of your questions.

Talking about questions, this book raises a lot of them, and provides the insight needed to help answer them. There are many perplexing questions in the arena of healing. For instance, if the promise of healing in the Scriptures are so clear as in James 5:15 "….the prayer of faith will heal the sick…", why is it that the cases of recovery through prayer and faith are not 100%? If God is compassionate, merciful and all powerful, then what are the obstacles to His healing power? The crucial question is; Does God desire perfect health for all? If He does, why are some healed and others not? How can we overcome the obstacles to healing and obtain more results? You can find out right now…..

Chapter 2

The Questions On Your Mind
What are the difficult questions?

C.S. Lewis, the renowned theologian and author of the celebrated book *The Lion, the Witch and the Wardrobe*, in another book titled *A Grief Observed* (written after the death of his wife) reacts to his personal suffering and loss through rage against God for taking his wife. His writings call into question the benefit of prayer, the love of God, His goodness and willingness to help the desperate in a time of need. His book describes the human heart as crying out, unable to conceive how a loving God could be without compassion[1]. Can God's love be so different from human love as to be a complete mystery? Doesn't His word say; "can a mother forget her suckling child, or have no compassion and tender loving care for the child of her womb? Even if she should forget, I will never forget you" (Is 49:15, paraphrased). Is the compassion of Jesus towards the sick not a truthful reflection of the love of

God towards the sick today? So why does it sometimes appear that He is unmoved at man's desperate plea for healing?

The starting point for tackling any challenge begins not with the ability to solve the problem, but with defining the problem. Albert Einstein said; "the formulation of a problem is sometimes more important than its solution". Asking the right questions helps to bring more clarity and illumination about a subject matter. When God asked Adam in the garden "Adam where are you....have you eaten of the fruit...?" He was not asking these questions because He did not know where Adam was, or what he had done, He was asking these questions so that Adam could locate himself, clearly identify his position and come to terms with the full reality of his current situation. In this chapter questions are used in a similar way – to identify our position and clarify our true beliefs, so we can be raised to a position where we are able to receive God's answers to our questions.

Healing is a perplexing subject, the more answers you discover, the more questions you generate. Healing for the purpose of this book is defined as an instant or gradual restoration of bodily strength and function after a time of weakness, disease or injury, with or without the use of medical intervention.

Questions, Questions and more Questions!

Children just love to ask questions, my kids ask so many questions, sometimes I get irritated. But asking questions is not a bad thing, in fact it should be encouraged because that is one of the ways children (and adults) learn best. The questions asked here help to shed light on the subject at hand and lay a foundation for the answers in subsequent chapters. God is not unnerved by an inquiring mind, nor is He irritated by a sincere question, so we can ask in faith and without fear. The questions range from general, academic, to the issue of God's sovereignty, and are grouped as such.

General Questions

- Is healing available to every believer?
- How can I receive healing if it is available?
- Why is the subject of divine healing a source of confusion and division in the church?
- What is the role of my faith for my healing?
- Do we need more faith or more power for healing?
- What is the place of persistent prayer?
- Why would the Holy Spirit, who healed the sick before His advent, not continue to do so today during his era which began at Pentecost. Has the Miracle Worker (the Holy Spirit) done away with the healing miracles during His own dispensation today?
- Does the fact that Christ could do no miracle at Nazareth, except heal a few sick folk because of their unbelief (Mark 6:5-6), imply that even when God's desire is clearly to heal, some might not be healed because of unbelief?
- Would it be right to conclude that because of the failure of Christ's disciples to heal the boy with the unclean spirit, (Matt 17:14-2) that it was not the will of God to heal him?
- If, as some suggest, it is God's will for some to remain in sickness, then would not every doctor, nurse and medical personnel be defying the will of God as they tried to bring a cure? Would every hospital or clinic not be a house of rebellion instead of a house of mercy?
- If sin and disobedience bring sickness and disease today just as in the Old Testament, should not healing and restoration follow full repentance just as it did in the Old Testament times?
- If our bodies are the temple of the Holy Spirit, does He not care and prefer His human temples in best repair just as the inward man?
- Why is it that some whom God has used powerfully in the healing ministry died of sickness or disease? E.g. Elisha, after healing many, died of sickness, even though

his dead bones still raised the dead.

Academic Questions

- Some theologians, ministers and scholars argue that the power to heal is historically conditioned and confined to the ministry of the apostles. Others take it for granted that the power to heal the sick, once given to the disciples by Jesus, was endowed to the church in principle. An important question must therefore be; has healing/miracles passed away with the early apostles?
- The atonement has been suggested as the warrant for healing[2,3]. But others say there is no bodily healing in the atonement[4,5,6,7]. Another question we must ask then is this, is physical healing included in the atonement?
- Mark16:18, Matt10:5-14, and Lk10:1-11 have been suggested as scriptural premise and authority for healing in the present day church[8]. Some scholars disagree, stating that the commission to the twelve and seventy (Matt10:5-14 and Lk10:1-11) was applicable only to the early apostles[9]. If this is true what relevance or value do the NT records of physical healing have for the guidance of Christian practice today? If they were factual accounts of physical healings, should we expect such healings to happen today in response to our prayer?
- If the healings and miracles of the first three centuries were real and useful then for the establishment of the church as some scholars argue[10], can we not argue that they would be equally useful in the church's evangelistic endeavours today?
- Have healing and miracles ceased with the apostolic era? If they have, on what grounds may we expect to receive healing in response to prayer, and on what basis did those healed by prayer or miracles obtain their healing?
- Is the book of Acts a revelation of the way the Holy

Spirit wants to continue to act in the church today?

- If miracles and healings passed away with the apostles, what is the purpose of the gifts of healing and miracles in the church today?

God's Sovereignty

- The question of the will and sovereignty of God as it relates to prayer for healing must also be answered. If the sovereignty of God is the deciding factor in whether healing is granted in response to prayer, what role does our prayer and faith play?
- Since God is all-powerful does that mean that sickness is God's will? Otherwise how do we explain the fact that sickness exists? Can one say "everything that exists is the way God wants it to be?"
- Does God use sickness as a "thorn in the flesh"?
- If Jesus healed all the sick that came to him based on compassion, why would he not do so today? Has he ceased to be compassionate or merciful?
- Does the Bible support the view that perfect health or healing is the will of God for everyone who prays for it, or does God allow some sickness, some of the time?
- If God healed in the past when sick people cried out to Him, why did he heal then? If He healed in response to a need, or because of his mercy, or for his glory are these reasons no longer valid today?

These and many others are questions this book will try to answer, and bring more understanding as we proceed through its pages.

Chapter 3

What Is The Case Against Healing?
*Why is there prejudice against healing
even in the Christian church?*

The story is told of a minister who did not believe God still healed today, and just to prove his point, he set out to demonstrate it. He claimed he had the gift of healing and invited those who needed healing to come forward to the altar to be healed. He knew in his heart that nothing would happen (at least so he thought) and that was exactly the point he wanted to prove. About thirty people came forward; they did not know that the minister did not believe in healing. He prayed like he had seen Oral Roberts (a popular healing evangelist) pray on TV; laying hands on the people and proclaiming loudly, "in the name of Jesus, be healed!" You know what happened? They were all healed (or seemed to be). He quickly explained it away as a cure by the power of suggestion. But there was a boy who came out with his arm in a sling but went back to his seat waving his arms and claiming he was cured, that really bothered the minister and spoiled the whole point of his sermon[11]. (God does have a sense of humour).

One of the greatest losses the church has suffered since her beginning has been the loss of her full heritage of healing power. This loss has come about through, I believe, the development of four main prejudices against healing. I have always been baffled by the resistance to the subject of healing within the church. So I put on my 'detective hat' and decided to investigate, (actually I decided to do a research project on this topic). I found four main different but overlapping views. The materialistic view, the idea that sickness is God's direct disciplinary gift, the dispensational view, and the existential view. (Not to worry I will explain each one).

The **Materialistic** view is based on the conviction that our bodies can be cared for adequately by medical and physical means alone, and that religious help is redundant. This "orthodox" medical point of view prevailed at the turn of the 20th century because of scientific breakthroughs and advances in the medical field. The materialistic view ignores and rationalises the supernatural elements of the Christian message, particularly the healings performed by Jesus and his followers. This position assumes the healing stories in the gospels were later additions to the scriptures by a more naive early church. Another approach was to suggest that the healings described in the NT were symbolic or allegories. This point of view claims to believe the New Testament while denying the reality of the healings and miracles within the New Testament[12].

The second case against healing is **the idea of sickness as God's direct disciplinary measure** or that sickness is a cross sent from God. This 16th century Christian view assumes that

God is responsible for sickness, that sickness is given as a correction and chastisement for breaking His commandments, and that sickness enables the sufferer to grow in faith and become more saintly. In other words sickness is good. Individuals may seek medical help, even though these actions are not quite consistent with this logic. This view is found in the English office of the visitation of the sick[13]. What happened during this period to diminish the church's belief in Christ's healing ministry is complex; but one of the main factors was that some unchristian philosophies (Platonic, Stoic, Manichean and asceticism) infected Christianity. These view points saw man's body as a prison that confines his spirit and hinders his spiritual growth. Christian perfection was defined as putting the body to death through suffering, mortification and penances. The body wars against the spirit, therefore it is an enemy to be subdued through punishment, rather than an ally to be healed[14]. From this thinking it is easy to understand why sickness was viewed as God's disciplinary gift to help the believer become more saintly. To an extent this stoic, unchristian view of the body still affects the thinking of many Christians today. Reflected in this attitude is a kind of spiritual schizophrenia; Christian doctors and nurses work to make the patient well, obeying Christ's injunctions to help the sick and needy. On the contrary, some preachers sometimes persuade the patient that acceptance of this cross is Christ's basic message. If the patient recovers through medicine, this is deemed acceptable; but God is somehow portrayed as mysteriously desiring man to suffer in a redemptive way. Little wonder, then, that in many segments of the church, when disaster strikes it is referred to as God's will.

The third view against healing is the **Dispensational view**; the belief that God originally gave the early church such ministries as healing, in order to establish his church and validate the first apostles, and that thereafter miracles ceased, (the cessation theory). In the early twentieth century, the strongest, and in many ways most influential person to affirm the cessation of miracles was Benjamin Warfield, a Princeton theologian. In 1918 Warfield's book *Counterfeit Miracles* was published. It stated that miracles were part of the credentials of the apostles as the authoritative agents of God in founding the church, and that they passed away with the early apostles. Warfield concluded that the power of working miracles was not extended beyond the disciples upon whom the apostles conferred it by the imposition of their hands. After these men passed off the scene, there could be no more miracles. Warfield also claimed that as a matter of historical fact, miracles have not continued beyond the apostolic period. He argued that claims of the continuation of miracles into the post apostolic period (ca 100-150) are unfounded. This theory was mostly embraced by the more conservative churches that cherished the historical value of the New Testament, but found that certain elements such as the healing ministry no longer existed in their churches. This was then explained by stating that God gave a special dispensation for these mighty works only for a particular period and purpose. This was the view of reformation giants such as Luther[15] and Calvin[16]. Another theologian (Robert Anderson) stated that "signs and wonders" were not guaranteed to us, as in Pentecostal days, and miracles had ceased after the apostles. Yet another theologian (Wade Boggs) presented this same thesis; he said "there is no doubt that healing was central to the ministry of Jesus, and his disciples carried on his work of healing the sick, but this was only a dispensation for the period of the New Testament, and has no application to our time."[18, 19]

The fourth case against healing is the **"Existential" theory**; this theory discards any idea of a supernatural non-physical reality existing in the material world. It questions the value of history, and believes as the truth, a scientific understanding of the world as a closed and totally physical system. This theory suggests that the course of nature cannot be broken into, or interrupted by God, or any power beyond physical "existence"[20, 21]. Bultmann, a highly regarded German theologian, described the gospel account of healing as "mythology". These events, he maintains, did not take place in actual fact, but were created by the faith of the early Christian community. Christian healing therefore has no place in today's Christianity[22].

The existence of counterfeit miracles is also a reason why some shy away from the possibility of miracles. There is a concern about Christians being deceived by false miracles or false miracle workers. Another argument against healing is that it is wrong to seek for signs and wonders based on Matt 12:39. In the next chapter we shall discover if any of these arguments against healing have any real basis.

Chapter 4

Refuting The Case Against Healing
*Does the prejudice against healing
have any scriptural Basis?*

I think it is fair to say that every time Jesus met with infirmity, spiritual or physical, he treated it as an enemy. Every time a sick person came to him in faith, Jesus healed that person. Jesus treats sickness as a manifestation of the kingdom of Satan which he had come to destroy. Nowhere in the gospels do we see Christ encouraging the sick to bear their cross of sickness and live with their illness. Yet there are many people – good Christian people – who are suffering and broken. Is there any value or purpose in this kind of suffering?

Is sickness a cross that some must carry?
In order to answer this question we must understand that

there is a kind of brokenness that all men suffer on their way to wholeness, but there is another kind of suffering or brokenness which is destructive and renders a man unfit to obey the great commandment of loving God and neighbour. Their inner turmoil prevents them from carrying out God's will, and yet paradoxically, they may still believe that such a sickness is God's will. For instance a person suffering from mental depression will find it hard to believe in God's love for him. He would not be able to respond to God or his neighbour in love. Those with a "cross" centred spirituality find it difficult to ask for relief from pain - healing would take away their opportunity to carry their cross and imitate Jesus. Jesus tells his followers to bear their cross daily; yet, whenever he meets people who are sick, he reaches out and cures them. Was he inconsistent, or have we misunderstood his words? There is a clear distinction between the two kinds of suffering: the cross that Jesus carried was the cross of persecution, the kind of suffering that comes from outside a man because of the wickedness of evil men. The suffering that Jesus is against, which he himself did not endure, and which he referred to as the works of the devil, was sickness. This kind of suffering, whether physical, or emotional, is destructive because it tears man apart from within. This twofold distinction is clear in the life of Jesus. There is a marked contrast between Jesus' attitude to persecution, and his reaction to sickness and demonic possession.

The uncompromising stance of Jesus towards sickness is clear, and is reiterated in his commission to the twelve disciples in Luke 9, and the seventy-two in Luke 10. We can also see the attitude of the early church; disease is an evil thing – not a blessing sent by God. Moreover, the mandate to all believers to preach the gospel promises healing as a sign that will follow those who believe (Mk 16:18).

To say that God desires men to be healed of their sickness does not connote a Christianity without a cross. Suffering through sickness is seen as evil by Jesus Christ - an evil to be overcome when it appears to overwhelm and destroy the inner life of a man; however suffering should be endured and embraced when it comes from the persecution of an evil world, or from the burdens of our labour for God. Although good can result from it, suffering is in itself the result of sin; it is only to be endured for the sake of the kingdom and not for its own sake.

Suffering is a mystery that we all have to wrestle with in some form or another. If God can put an end to all suffering, why doesn't he do so, we ask? There are no simple answers to the timeless question; 'why do the innocent suffer'? What can be said, however, is that in general, God desires that we be healthy rather than sick. Sickness is in itself evil, although good may result from it. Sickness is not directly willed by God, but as a result of the original sin, it is permitted.

It is true that some sickness may have a higher purpose. Sometimes it serves to chastise and bring us to our senses, at other times, it may turn us around and redirect our lives into a better course. However by New Testament standards, it should be normative for the Christian to pray for the removal of sickness rather than accept it. Redemptive sickness (sickness which has a redeeming value) is the exception, not the rule. It is vital that we discard an erroneous attitude towards suffering. Otherwise our experience will be a negative self-fulfilling prophecy which says; 'Blessed are those who expect nothing, for they shall not be disappointed'. If we believe that the ordinary will of God is that sick persons should raise their suffering to the level of the cross, and accept pain rather than try to rid themselves of it, then such people would feel guilty about praying for healing which would be tantamount to trying to escape the cross[23]. Let us understand and observe that God desires wholeness for us, we are his temple, his workmanship created for good works. Let us not glory in sickness anymore; even God cannot pluck a broken harp.

Only for Apostles?

The argument that miracles ceased with the apostles (cessation theory) is untrue. In the book of Acts we find many non-apostles (Stephen in Acts 6:8, The seventy-two in Luke 10:9, Ananias Acts 9:10-18) working miracles and healing the sick. The miraculous gifts of the Spirit, including signs and wonders were not limited to the Apostles. Neither by example nor statement of Scripture can anyone prove that the miraculous gifts were limited to the Apostles. The attempt, therefore, to connect the alleged cessation of the gifts with the passing of the apostles is futile. Miracles did not authenticate the Apostles, miracles authenticated Jesus Christ (John 14:11) and the Gospel message.

In line with 1Cor 12:28 – "God has appointed in the church... works of miracles", that miracles may continue. This divine appointment of miracle working was never meant to be for apostolic times only but for the church throughout its history. Hence the cessation of miracles is never the Lord's doing but represents failure on the part of God's people. The staggering promise in John 14:12 carries us far beyond negative views in regard to the continuation of miracles into an entirely new arena. It is not a question of whether miracles happen but whether we have begun to witness what Christ intends. Could it be that our faith is yet still too small?[24]

False Healers and Miracles

Concerning Christians being deceived by false miracles or false miracle workers/bogus faith healers, a few points based on scripture may be made in this regard. It is true that there are false miracles Exo 7:11, 22, Acts 8:9-11. Such claims however should not rule out the real thing. Does not the counterfeit actually imply the existence of the valid? It is inconsistent or odd when most miracles are ascribed to Satan while none are ascribed to God. (The Pharisees said about Jesus, that His miracles were not from God and that He cast out demons by the prince of demons). God is the All-powerful miracle worker, Satan is only a counterfeiter. The identity of these false miracle workers is always known through their denial of the Gospel. There is no indication anywhere in scripture that genuine Christians with the Holy Spirit in them will work false miracles. Paul gives reassurance in the New Testament when he says "no one can say Jesus is Lord except by the Holy Spirit (1Cor 12:3). This should reassure us that if we see those who make a genuine profession of faith, believe in the incarnation and deity of Christ (1John 4:2), and show the fruit of the Holy Spirit in their lives and bear fruit in their ministry, we should not be suspicious that they are false miracle workers, but should be thankful to God that the Holy Spirit is working, even in those who may not hold exactly the same convictions that we do on every point of doctrine. Indeed if God waited to work miracles only through those who are perfect in both doctrine and conduct of life, no miracles would be worked until Christ returns[25].

Seeking for signs

By New Testament standards, it should be normal for the Christian to pray for healing or even miracles if necessary. The argument that a wicked and perverse generation seeks for a miraculous sign is out of context in this case. Jesus said these words to insincere people who were only out to test Him. These were the Pharisees and Sadducees (Matt16:4, Luke11:16, Matt16:1; Mark8:11) who did not believe in Him despite His miracles and who continually pressured Him to prove Himself as one sent by God, just as in the temptations by the devil in Matt 4:4. What Jesus was reprimanding in these passages was not a desire for miracles but the demand for signs from an evil and unbelieving heart. If it is wrong to desire miracles or pray for them, then Acts 4:29-31, 5:12; a prayer for miraculous signs, with an immediate response from God would be terribly out of place. Another passage that encourages the desire for spiritual gifts which includes miracles is 1Cor 12:31, 14:1, 39, where Paul admonished us to earnestly desire spiritual gifts.

When signs and supernatural phenomena are lacking in our churches, we need to examine ourselves. In the Old Testament for example, an absence of the miraculous is not taken as normal for the people of God; rather it is seen as a sign of judgement. Psalm 74:1-9 states;

> *Why have you rejected us forever, O God? Why does your anger smoulder against the sheep of your pasture?.....We are given no miraculous signs; no prophets are left, and none of us knows how long this will be" (NIV)*

The Psalmist takes the absence of the miraculous as the judgement of God. He refuses to accept the absence of God's supernatural deeds as normal living conditions for the people of God, contrary to what the modern day cessationist will have us believe. In Psalm 77:7-10 despite the absence of miracles the Psalmist refers to God as "the God who *performs* miracles" (v14) not the God who *performed* miracles. The Psalmist used a present tense participle, which meant that God was still doing miracles. The fact that Israel was not experiencing these miracles was a sign of God's displeasure, not an indication that God was no longer performing them[26].

Chapter 5

Interpreting Scripture
How do you read Scripture?

Someone once said if you take a 'text' out of 'context' you end up with a 'con' (witty words indeed). It seems that some of the differences of opinion in the church about healing and miracles depend on how we interpret Scripture. Before we begin to look at the scriptural evidence for healing let us take a crash course in hermeneutics (the science of interpretation of scripture).

In order to interpret Scripture rightly we must follow certain principles, a couple will be discussed here:

While we must acknowledge that all Scripture is inspired by God (2 Tim 3:16), when we formulate our doctrines, our starting point must be from the clear teaching of Scripture. Illustrations or analogies must then be fitted into that which Scriptures state explicitly. Although a Scripture will have a specific meaning within its historical context, the spiritual truth of that verse could have varied applications for us today. In hermeneutic lingo, there is a term called 'principalising'. It is a legitimate hermeneutical way of showing the contemporary relevance of the narrative portions of Scripture for today's Christian. Principalising is an attempt to discover the spiritual, moral, or theological principles in a narrative that have relevance for the contemporary believer. It is a method of trying to understand a story in such a way that we can recognise the original reason it was included in Scripture, i.e. the principles it was meant to teach. It is unlike allegorising, which gives a story new meaning by assigning its details symbolic significance that the original author did not intend[27].

In Acts for example, a crucial hermeneutical question is whether biblical narratives that describe what happened in the early church should also function as the norm for today's church. For historical precedent to be the norm, it must be related to intent.[28] This simply means that we can only interpret the healing narratives in Acts or the Gospels as illustrations of what should happen in the church today if we can establish that this was intended by the authors. When we look at the clear teaching in James 5:14-16, John 14:12-14, Mark 16:16-18 etc. there is no doubt that the healing narratives in the Gospels and Acts describe what should be the pattern for the church today.

Some theologians say we cannot determine the doctrine of healing or what should be the norm for church life based on the narratives in the Gospels or Acts. If that is the case what then is the relevance of Christ's healing ministry for us? The argument against using these narratives as sources of a doctrine on healing is totally invalid because theologians since the reformation have always used it for doctrine. The Gospel and Acts are major sources of doctrine for missions, evangelism, Christology etc. What this argument really means is that we may not use them to determine doctrine about healing and miracles for today's church. This is simply reading or interpreting Scripture with an anti-supernatural bias. In other words they say you can copy any non-supernatural elements of the Gospels and Acts, but you are not free to use the supernatural elements in the same way. Another reason why this argument is invalid is because in bible times, especially in the Ancient Near East which includes Israel, the most common way of teaching or perpetuating tradition or theology was by telling a story. The Gospel 'stories' were written to communicate theology. Recent scholarly discussions in narrative theology ought to eliminate this argument forever.[29] Much of the Old and New Testament consists of narrative literature, which if the argument were true would mean we would have to discard a large percentage of the Scriptures as doctrinally worthless. The reality is that nobody follows this line of reasoning. It only means you cannot use the Gospels and Acts to determine the relevance of miracles for the church's present ministry, and this is a teaching not based on the bible, but on personal prejudice. This reason also falls flat on its face because "All Scripture is given by inspiration of God, and is profitable for doctrine, for reproof, for correction, for instruction in righteousness" (2 Tim 3:16). Paul encourages Christians to follow his example as he follows Christ. We are to follow their righteous living as well as their miraculous ministry. When we stumble as we follow Christ in the walk of righteousness, we rise up and keep on walking. In the same manner, when we fail to obtain results in the healing ministry, we must arise again and keep applying ourselves in faith with patience.

Revelation is progressive - truths in the Old Testament types and shadows become increasingly clearer as we proceed through the Gospels and Epistles. The New Testament is the definitive commentary on the Old Testament, and the Holy Spirit is the ultimate authority on proper context, meaning, and application. Only through Him can we receive the knowledge of the truth (John 16:13).

What colour are your sunglasses?

All of us are influenced in our thinking, by our traditions, education, culture etc. These factors unwittingly 'tint' or influence our ideas more than we realise, and affect the way we read Scripture. For instance the teaching that the age of miracles is past has been so established in some quarters of the Christian church that, many, while reading the Scriptures, thoughtlessly pass over the biblical teaching on healing, believing that it is not applicable to our day. We must never allow the bible to become an archaic book of long gone mighty deeds of God. If we come to the Scriptures with the assumption that miracles have passed away, then this will colour our perception when we read about them. Instead of praising God for the miracles, we reason; 'that does not happen today'. However if you come with the presupposition that miracles are possible and available in all ages, then when you read about the miracles you will exclaim in excitement "praise God, if it happened then, it can happen now, God is no respecter of persons, Jesus Christ is the same yesterday, today and for ever".

Scriptures used to support the doctrine of ceasation of miracles are misinterpreted e.g. 1Cor13:8-10, 1Cor12:7,25, 28-30 14:5,12,26 Eph 4:12. This doctrine rejects and contradicts the testimony of the early church Fathers. Even if miracles did dwindle away during the dark ages as the spiritual condition of the church deteriorated, it does not mean they entirely ceased. And if they did even cease because of the church's doctrinal defection and spiritual depravity, could they not reappear if the church, or any group within it, should return to spiritual fidelity and purity. It is a serious error indeed to relegate miracles to the past. It is sad to hear among some who affirm the message of salvation, and the need for regeneration, that miracles are not to be expected any longer. If through the proclamation of the word in the power of the Spirit, the miracle of rebirth can and does occur; will not that same Spirit also work other "signs and wonders"[30]?

In order to excuse the absence of healing and miracles in their experience, some Christians misinterpret Scripture, then come up with conclusions which merely reveal their irrational unwillingness to accept God's Word as it is, and bring their own masked powerlessness to be judged at the bar of Holy Writ!

In the absence of statements in the Scriptures which specify that miracles, signs and wonders will pass away, the cessationism theory collapses under the weight of miracles, signs and wonders from Genesis to Revelation, and to the present day. We shall now cross examine the witnesses.

Chapter 6

The Old Testament Legacy Of Healing

Can today's church lay claim to the Old Testament healing covenant?

The king was grievously ill, there was heaviness in the air, the prophet had spoken - the disease was terminal. The professional mourners were preparing the royal lament, the council elders deliberating on the king's successor, and the imperial household was in deep distress. The king was deflated, dejected and discouraged because of his impending untimely demise. Unable to bear the anguish and turmoil any longer he cried to the Lord to heal him. He pleaded his case, broke down in tears and wept sore before the Lord. He did not want to die, not yet, not now. God heard his prayers, healed him and gave him many more years of life. (2Kings 20:1-7)

2kings 20:5;

> *Turn again, and tell Hezekiah the captain of my people,*
> *Thus saith the Lord, the God of David thy father, I have*
> *heard your prayers, I have seen thy tears: behold I will*
> *heal thee: on the third day thou shalt go up unto the*
> *house of the Lord.*

After King Hezekiah's fervent prayer for his recovery, the prophet Isaiah asked his attendant to take a lump of figs and apply it to the boil; resulting in the king's recovery (2kings 20:7). The account of Hezekiah's sickness includes one of the rare references to herbal treatment in the Old Testament.

In this chapter we shall examine passages from the Old Testament as a backdrop for the healing ministry of Christ and the apostles in the subsequent chapters.

The Old Testament Healing Foundation Scripture
Soon after the miraculous deliverance of the children of Israel from Egypt (Exodus 14:21-31), God revealed Himself as the Healer of His people.

Exodus 15:26

> ..... *If thou wilt diligently hearken to the voice of the*
> *Lord thy God, and wilt do that which is right in his*
> *sight, and wilt give ear to his commandments, and keep*
> *all his statutes, I will put none of these diseases upon*
> *thee, which I have brought upon the Egyptians: for I*
> *am the Lord that healeth thee.*

This verse is the foundation for healing in the Old Testament. The last clause of the verse translates one of the covenant names of the God of Israel, Yahweh – Rephucha - 'The Lord your healer'. There are four points to be noted about this promise to keep the people of Israel healthy which the Lord made at Marah. First of all, healing was conditionally promised upon their obedience. Secondly, the promise is primarily of the prevention of disease, and therefore, preservation of health. Thirdly, this promise implies that disobedience opens people up to disease. Finally, the people are assured that if they do suffer disease, the Lord is able to heal them. The primary intention of this promise is the preservation of good health. This is made clearer in another promise.

Deut 7:15

> *"And the Lord will take away from thee all sickness, and will put none of the evil diseases of Egypt, which thou knowest, upon thee; but will lay them upon all them that hate thee".*

The way for the people of God to preserve their health is to obey the commands and statutes of the Lord which really are designed to promote and maintain health (Prov 3:7-8, 4:22). The Jewish physician Sussman Muntner estimated that 'out of the 613 biblical commands and prohibitions, at least 213 are health rules in the form of rigorously observed ceremonial rites[31].

We know that when his people became ill, whether through disobedience or not, the Lord did heal them (Psalm 30:2, 103:3, 107:19-20) The primary meaning and derivation of the word Rapha in the Old Testament is 'restoration to wholeness and normality' with regards to health and disease. It also refers to the Lord as Israel's healer - in the broadest possible sense. The claim of the Lord to be the healer of his people should not be taken to mean that they would have no need of human physicians for their treatment of disease and sickness. It is in opposition to the claims of foreign deities that the Lord asserts that he is the real Healer of His people, not in opposition to doctors or medicine[32].

The Psalmist's song

From Psalm 103 we note that God is beneficial, and among the benefits his people can expect to enjoy are; forgiveness of all sins, healing of all diseases, restoration of strength, and redemption from destruction. If we have no doubts that He "forgives all our sins" then we can equally assume that God is willing to heal all our diseases. The mercy of healing is as universal a privilege as the mercy of forgiveness. Also God desires not only to heal us but to renew us to better health. The eagle referred to in this Psalm is a long-lived bird. When it is nearly a hundred years old (besides its annual molting) it casts off all its feathers, from head to talons, and undergoes a complete re-feathering. As far as I know the eagle is unique in this respect; which is why the Psalmist used it for his illustration.

Psalm 103:2-5

> Bless the Lord, O my soul, and forget not all his benefits: Who forgiveth all thine iniquities; who healeth all thy diseases; Who redeemeth thy life from destruction; who crowneth thee with lovingkindness and tender mercies; Who satisfieth thy mouth with good things; so that thy youth is renewed like the eagle's.

Psalm 30:2-3, (TLB)

> O Lord ...I pleaded with you, and you gave me my health again. You brought me back from the brink of the grave, from death itself, and here I am alive!

The Great Redemption Passage

Isaiah 53:5 (Matt8:17, 1Peter2:24)

> But he was wounded for our transgressions, he was

bruised for our iniquities: the chastisement of our peace
was upon him; and with his stripes we are healed.

We must realise from the onset that sickness came as a result
of the fall of Adam, and illness and disease are simply part of
the outworking of the curse after the fall, and will eventually
lead to physical death. However, Christ redeemed us from
that curse when he died on the cross - "... he took our
infirmities and carried our sorrows... By his wounds we are
healed" (Isaiah 53:4-5). This passage clearly refers to both
physical and spiritual healing that Christ purchased for us.
1Peter 2:24 and Matthew 8:16-17 both quote Isaiah 53:4, not
just with reference to freedom from sin, but to physical
healing. In the atonement, Christ has purchased for us not
only complete freedom from sin but also from physical
weakness and infirmity in his work of redemption. At his
coming (1Cor 15:23) we shall receive perfect resurrection
bodies no longer subject to disease or sickness, but for now
when we find ourselves afflicted by sickness, we can expect
the prayer of faith to heal the sick. We can expect the gift of
healings to bring healing in our lives and we can fully expect
that God will grant us a foretaste of that perfect disease-free
resurrection body as demonstrated by the healing miracles of
Jesus. Also the ministry of healing seen in the lives of the
apostles and others in the early church would indicate that
this was part of the ministry of the new covenant age.
Through His life and ministry Christ destroyed the works of
the devil in the form of sickness, disease and oppression.
Through his death He dealt the fatal and final blow to sin,
which is the root of all sickness, disease and oppression.

Healing of all forms of sickness is taken in Matthew to be the
fulfilment of what Isaiah prophesied of the Servant of the
Lord. According to FF Bosworth, the Hebrew verbs for *bear*
used in the Isaiah 53 text, when used of sin (vv11-12), signify
"to assume as a heavy burden and to bear away the guilt of sin
as one's own"; that is to bear sin as a mediator in order to

atone for it. But in verse 4, where not sins but our sicknesses and pains are the object, the mediatory sense remains the same. What this means is that Christ did not merely enter into the fellowship of our sufferings, but He took upon Himself the sufferings that we had to bear and deserved to bear; and therefore He not only bore them away, but endured them in order to discharge us from them. When one takes the suffering of another upon himself, not merely in fellowship with him but in his stead, this is called substitution. Therefore the bearing and removal of human disease is an integral part of the redeeming work of Christ. Since our substitute bore our sins and sickness, we do not have to bear them[33].

The fact of healing in the atonement necessitates the continuation of Christ's healing ministry today. Accordingly, He gives the above promise to do the same and "greater works" in answer to our prayers. As long as the church has remained under the control of the Spirit, the works have continued; and history reveals "that whenever we find a revival of primitive faith and apostolic simplicity, there we find the evangelical miracles which surely characterised the apostolic age"[34].

Can today's church lay claim to the Old Testament healing covenant?

Sickness is part of the curse of the law (Deut 28:15-68), but Galatians 3:13 says "Christ hath redeemed us from the curse of the law, being made a curse for us: for it is written, cursed is every one that hangeth on a tree". Christ was born under the law to redeem us from its curse. On the cross, Jesus bore the curse, became accursed and redeemed us from sickness, disease as well as other curses of the law.

The promises of God in Christ Jesus are yes and amen (paraphrased), so states Paul in 2Corinthians 1:18-20. This passage, I believe, means that in our Lord Jesus Christ, all the promises of God made under the old covenant, i.e. throughout the Old Testament scriptures, are now our blood-sealed legacy. They are ours now, in Him, and may be appropriated with boldness and confidence. Every promise is ours in Christ. "His divine power hath given unto us......exceeding great and precious promises" (2Peter 1:3-4). Even the so called kingdom promises, made originally to the covenant nation Israel, are now the shared possession of us Gentile Christians; for in Christ we have become incorporated into the true Israel. All the divine pledges given through the Abrahamic and Davidic covenants; are now ours. This bestowing of Old Testament promises to Christian believers has a powerful bearing on the subject of divine healing of the body[35].

Those who were not cured

There are some cases of those who were not cured in the Old Testament; the Son of Jereboam 1 (1Kings 15:29), Ahaziah (2Kings 1:2,16), Gehazi (2King 5:27), and Uzziah (2Chronicles 26:19-29). These four were not cured due to personal or family sin. In the cases of personal sin, the sickness was part of their punishment. In its explanation of the meaning and purpose behind the human experience of disease, the Old Testament is concerned to make two essential points; the first is that God is in control of all natural phenomena whatever their nature, and secondly, that he can use their occurrences and effects in the training and discipline of his people.

With the testimony of these scriptures from the old covenant days, now made even more evident through the new covenant, we now survey the New Testament evidence.

Chapter 7

The Healing Ministry Of Jesus
*Can the church replicate the healing
ministry of Christ?*

Miss JS of Philadelphia had a mysterious, agonising and chronic disease that had crippled and made her suffer deeply. She began to lay claim to God's promise for bodily healing, and began experiencing slight indications of his power in several partial reliefs. Eventually she decided to ask God for a total recovery. (The story is narrated from the patient's view point.) 'The evening was devoted to prayer, led by her Pastor. Her physician was present as well as a few Christian brothers and sisters. Some of them left as evening approached while others tarried. Up to this point there had not been oneness of mind in the gathering. The patient asked those who remained, "can you tarry with me till morning if need be? I feel it must be by waiting that our Father will give us this blessing. Are you of one mind in this matter?" Those who stayed behind gathered round her chair. Never can that little group forget that night; they continued to wait (pray) before the Lord. Occasionally, one or another would quote and comment on an appropriate scripture, or engage in brief audible prayer. The sick woman lay in quiet expectancy with a remarkable sense of the divine presence, and in deep communion with the Heavenly Father. Before midnight the patient felt led to vocally offer herself to God in fresh consecration. Up to this point she was still in pain and very weak. After a brief silence there suddenly flashed before her a vivid view of the healing of the man with the withered arm from the Gospels (Mark 3:1 Luke 6:6). At the same time the Holy Spirit impressed upon her heart the faith to claim a similar blessing. It seemed as if the heavens were at a moment opened, and she was conscious of a baptism of strength, as sensibly and as positively as if an electric shock had passed through her system. Feeling the strength come into her back, and into her helpless limbs, she laid her hands on the arms of the chair and pulled herself to a sitting posture. Her friends tried to assist her but this was not necessary - she stood up on her feet. Some were so startled they screamed. One of the brothers placed his hand upon her head and said 'Praise God from whom all blessings flow.' Miss JS' first thought was - can I kneel? So she tried to, and she did so as naturally as if she had been accustomed to it. The group poured out their souls in silent thanksgiving and praise; Miss JS walked around the room and sat down in a rocking chair with no pain or otherwise unpleasant sensations. She felt like her limbs and body were made new"[36].

Some Christians see the healing miracles solely as illustrations of Christ's teaching about the power and coming of the kingdom of God in the future, instead of displays of the very kingdom of God actually breaking into our present reality. This is largely due to a reluctance to recognise the presence of the supernatural element in the gospel accounts of Jesus. Even where the accounts of healing miracles are accepted, there is still a tendency to try to explain them in naturalistic terms, rather than admit their supernatural character[37].

A full understanding of the liberating, healing, saving message of Jesus Christ demands that we investigate whether he has come to free us even in this life from all sickness and disease. The proof of salvation was that men were being saved, restored to all that they had lost. A concept or doctrine of healing without the healing taking place is empty rhetoric. To deny or minimise the healing ministry is to take away much of the power of the gospel, and to leave in its stead a body of truths devoid of life.

Although the gospels abound with accounts of healings, why do many Christians find it so hard to believe that healing can still take place? If we get a new convert, (with no prior knowledge of Christian doctrine or history) to read the New Testament for a week, he would arrive at the conclusion or belief that the church consistently experiences and works miracles. It would take a theologian without the experience of the miraculous, but with a bias against miracles, to convince this young convert otherwise.

Having dispelled the arguments against the relevance of miracles for the church's present ministry, we can now look at the miracles/healing of Jesus in their true light.

The crippled woman

Luke13:11-13

> And, behold, there was a woman which had a spirit of infirmity eighteen years, and was bowed together, and could in no wise lift up her self. And when Jesus saw her, he called her to him, and said unto her, woman, thou art loosed from thine infirmity. And he laid his hands on her: and immediately she was made straight, and glorified God.

In Luke 13:16 Jesus describes this woman as a daughter of Abraham, bound by Satan for eighteen years. His healing of the woman on the Sabbath day raised criticism from the synagogue ruler. Jesus' reply to the criticism is very insightful, and teaches us a lot about his view of healing. His argument was that if on a Sabbath day you untie the bond which has confined your animals in order to allow them drink, how much more is it necessary to untie the bond of this woman who has been bound by Satan for eighteen years. Jesus' reference to the bond of Satan does not mean that this woman was demon possessed but that her condition was due to the activity of Satan as the primary cause of sin and disease[38]. The main reason for the choice of the case of the crippled woman, and its contribution to the New Testament view of healing, is its clear implication that disease can be directly attributed to Satan, and the cure or healing is therefore an illustration of the power of God over evil and over Satan. This power is demonstrated in the life, death and resurrection of Jesus Christ. This account of healing reveals the merciful, compassionate heart of our Lord towards his helpless and suffering children. The woman had no help and possibly no hope, and the hostile response of the synagogue ruler shows that the attitude of the religious leaders of the day was less than compassionate. But Jesus saw the woman in the midst of the crowd, had mercy on her, and loosed her from the unbearable bond of infirmity.

The Bethesda paralytic
On most occasions when Jesus healed the sick, the gospel record tells us that they came to him, or were brought to him. In the case of the Bethesda paralytic, Jesus took the initiative as in the case of the woman above.

John 5:5-9

And a certain man was there, which had an infirmity thirty and eight years. When Jesus saw him lie, and knew that he had been now a long time in that case, he saith unto him, wilt thou be made whole? The impotent

> *man answered him, Sir, I have no man, when the water*
> *is troubled, to put me into the pool: but while I am*
> *coming, another steppeth down before me. Jesus saith*
> *unto him, Rise, take up thy bed, and walk. And*
> *immediately the man was made whole, and took up his*
> *bed, and walked; and on the same day was the Sabbath.*

When we look at the record of Christ's healing ministry we see that Jesus himself initiated the healing only in a few cases. The fact that our Lord so seldom took the initiative is significant. It is never recorded that he sought out the sick, only that he healed them when he saw them, or when they were brought to him. This should encourage us to go to God in prayer, in times of sickness, rather than assume God will heal us since He knows we are sick. The most interesting record of all in this regard is the healing of the paralysed man by the pool of Bethesda. Around the pool at Bethesda were five porches to shelter the sick people who gathered there because of the healing reputation of the waters. Jesus comes into their midst and chooses to heal only one of the multitude, and then withdraws quietly and quickly afterwards. True as this may be, it must be said that although he did not often take the healing initiative he never failed to heal anyone who was brought to him, or who came to him in faith. The question Jesus asked the paralytic is quite interesting - one could say Jesus asked him "do you really want to be well?" This question appears like a 'no-brainer', but the paralytic's answer reveals that there was a possibility that he might not actually want to be healed. He replies "I have no man to help me into the pool". It is possible the man preferred the comfort and profit of his paralytic state than to be cured and thus compelled to face a hard life of earning a living without the pity and sympathy he was accustomed to. Many patients, unknowingly, are in this state. They truthfully say they want to be healed, but there is an unconscious and much more powerful motive which makes them want illness[39]. This could be a hindrance to healing. Another insight from reading the entire story of the Bethesda paralytic is that sickness can be a result of sin. This man's sickness was caused by sin because Jesus says to him "now you have been made whole, sin no more lest a worse thing comes upon you".

The paralysed man

Mark 2:3-5,11-12

> *And they come unto him, bringing one sick of the palsy, which was borne of four. And when they could not come nigh unto him for the press, they uncovered the roof where he was: and when they had broken it up, they let down the bed wherein the sick of the palsy lay. When Jesus say their faith, he said unto the sick of the palsy, son thy sins be forgiven. I say unto thee, arise, and take up thy bed, and go thy way into thine house. And immediately he arose took up his bed, and went forth before them all; insomuch that they were all amazed, and glorified God, saying We never saw it on this fashion.*

This account is interesting because it shows the role faith plays in healing. In the case of the paralysed man, it appears that the faith referred to is that of the friends who brought him through the roof. When the paralysed man is lowered through the roof, we read that Jesus saw their faith (v.5) and said; 'son your sins are forgiven' and in v11 he says; 'arise and take up your bed', and the man was healed. Two points will be made here; (1) the relationship of sin to sickness, or the effect of forgiveness on healing and (2) the relationship of faith to healing. We have mentioned the relationship between sin and sickness above and we shall discuss it in more detail later. Here we will only discuss the relationship between faith and healing. From the actions of the friends of the sick man we note that Jesus saw their faith, which suggests that faith is not just something intangible or unseen, but faith includes action which can be seen. We can conclude here that faith in Jesus' ability and willingness to heal sickness brings wholeness to the sick. God heals in answer to faith, and that faith could be that of the healer or the sick or both.

The man full of leprosy

Mark 1:40-44 (Matt 8:2-4 Luke 5:12-14)

> *And there came a leper to him, beseeching him, and kneeling down to him, and saying unto him, if thou wilt, thou canst make me clean. And Jesus, moved with compassion, put forth his hand and touched him, and saith unto him, I will: be thou clean. And, as soon as he had spoken, immediately the leprosy departed from him, and he was cleansed.*

This account reveals that Jesus cleansed the leper because he was moved with compassion. Jesus banishes all doubt about his willingness to heal when he states emphatically "I am willing", (in contemporary terms – "you bet I want to") in addition he stretched out his hands and touched him. Christ's willingness to touch him is amazing considering that doing so would render him ceremonially unclean. The leper never doubted Christ's ability to heal him but he was not so sure about his willingness (how true of many sick today). Jesus replies emphatically, 'I am willing', and as if to further buttress this point Jesus touches him, this would have blown the leper away - it was much more than he had bargained for. Jesus was not just willing to heal him, he touched him, he accepted him, wow! This account contributes to our understanding of Christ's healing ministry by showing both our Lord's willingness to heal, and His compassion as one of the motives for healing.

The man with the withered hand

Mark3:1 (Luke 6:6)

> *And he entered again into the synagogue; and there*

was a man there which had a withered hand. And they watched him, whether he would heal him on the Sabbath day; that they might accuse him. And he saith to the man which had the withered hand, Stand forth. And he saith unto them, Is it lawful to do good on the Sabbath days or to do evil? To save life, or to kill? But they held their peace. And when he had looked round about on them with anger, being grieved for the hardness of their hearts, he saith unto the man, stretch forth thine hand. And he stretched it out: and his hand was restored whole as the other.

In this account, when Jesus entered the synagogue on a Sabbath day, the authorities watched to see whether he would heal the man with the withered hand. Jesus called out the man, turned to those who hoped to catch him breaking the Sabbath and said, "Is it against the law to do good, on the Sabbath day or to do evil; to save life or to kill"? But they said nothing. Christ was grieved to find them so obstinate and legalistic, even when a man's well being was at stake. He looked at them in anger (and probably disgust), and proceeded to heal the man.

The clear implication of all this is that healing is a good work, important enough so that ritual laws should not stand in the way. It is like pulling an ox or ass out of a pit – valuable enough to break the Sabbath to accomplish it. Just as the ox has a right to live, the human has the right to be alive and well. Human beings are valuable and whatever contributes to their restoration and health is also important. The laws of the Sabbath, made to protect human beings from being overworked, could and should be broken to show mercy and minister healing[40].

The epileptic boy
Matt17:15-21 (Mark 9:14-29; Luke 9:37-43)(NRSV)

... "Lord, have mercy on my son, for he is an epileptic

and he suffers terribly; he often falls into the fire and often into the water. And I brought him to your disciples, but they could not cure him." Jesus answered, "you faithless and perverse generation, how much longer must I be with you? How much longer must I be with you? How much longer must I put up with you? Bring him here to me." And Jesus rebuked the demon, and it came out of him, and the boy was cured instantly. Then the disciples came to Jesus privately and said, "Why could we not cast it out?" He said to them, "Because of your little faith. For truly I tell you, if you have faith the size of a mustard seed, you will say to this mountain, 'Move from here to there,' and it will move; and nothing will be impossible for you. But this kind does not come out except by prayer and fasting".

This healing account is very relevant to the question of why some are not healed. The father of this boy had brought his son to the disciples, but they were unable to heal him. The Father was distraught and cried to Jesus "....if you are able to do anything, have pity on us and help us." Jesus said to him, "If you are able! – All things can be done for the one who believes" (NRSV). Immediately the father of the child cried out, "I believe; help my unbelief!" (Mark 9:22-24). Jesus cast out the demon responsible for the sickness and healed the boy. There are several important lessons to learn from this healing account; 1) sometimes physical sickness can have a demonic/ spiritual root, 2) the fact that the disciples could not heal the boy did not mean that it was not God's will to heal him, 3) when we do not obtain healing immediately we should persist in seeking for healing. 4) The statement of the father of the sick boy - "I believe; help my unbelief!" suggests that faith mingled with unbelief is a hindrance to obtaining results. 5) The fact that the disciples had been successful in previous healing expeditions prior to this case, suggests that different levels of faith and 'prayer power' are required to obtain results in different cases, in this case their 'little faith' (v.18) was not sufficient to bring results. 6) The fact that the disciples questioned Jesus about why they were unable to cast out the demon and heal the boy means that they fully expected (and rightly so) that they would be able to do what Jesus could do. 7) Jesus' response to his disciples' question about their failure to heal the boy means that faith, and prayer, with fasting are important factors in bringing healing to the sick. It also underpins the fact that faith is connected with healing. 8) Jesus did not heal the boy because he was Jesus, and the disciples did not fail because they were disciples. The reason for failure was lack of, or insufficient faith and prayer. 9) We also learn that even with a mustard seed-sized faith, nothing will be impossible for the one who believes.

The man born blind

John 9:1-3, 6-7

> And as Jesus passed by, he saw a man which was blind from his birth. And the disciples asked him, saying, Master, who did sin, this man or his parents, that he was born blind? Jesus answered, neither hath this man sinned, nor his parents: but that the works of God should be made manifest in him. When he had thus spoken, he spat on the ground, and made clay of the spittle, and he anointed the eyes of the blind man with the clay, and said unto him, Go wash in the pool of Siloam, (which is by interpretation Sent.) He went his way therefore, and washed and came seeing.

The account begins as Jesus and his disciples leave the temple, where beggars sat and asked for alms. On this day, one particular blind man attracted the attention of Jesus and his disciples. He was well known as one who was born blind, and it was believed that nothing could be done to give him sight (John 9:32). The disciples asked Jesus, "who sinned, this man or his parents that he was born blind"? There are several implications of this question; it shows that the disciples assumed that the man's blindness was due to sin. This shows the popular mindset and attitude of the day—that sickness was a punishment for sin. Jesus' reply must have confounded them - "neither this man nor his parents". There is no doubt that there is a connection between sin and disease because there would be no disease or calamity in the world if there were no sin, but the connection is not necessarily immediate and personal. Judaism affirmed that sickness was the result of sin and that it was one of God's punishments for disobedience to divine law. While it is easy to see how people arrived at the idea that sickness can be caused by defiance or unconscious trespass against God, this is no reason, as the book of Job shows, to assert that all sickness is caused by sin. In Luke 13:2-5 Jesus taught the same lesson – people who suffered tragedy were no more sinful than other people. When Jesus saw a need to speak of sin in connection with a sickness he did so. He believed that people sometimes fell into the hands of a force of evil in the world, which was hostile to God and righteousness, and that this was a primary cause of sickness. It seems that missing the moral and religious mark (sin) does leave an individual more open to the invasion of this evil power, but Jesus did not discuss this relationship in detail[41].

There are lessons we can learn from the disciples' comments i.e. the man's blindness was due to sin and his condition was incurable. These presuppositions were wrong. The result was, they asked the wrong questions and if Jesus had not been with them, there would have been no healing. It is interesting to note that the Pharisees also asked some questions. They questioned the genuineness of the healing, its lawfulness, and the meaningfulness of the miracle. We can learn a few more lessons from their questions and comments. We learn that healing comes from God - this was why the Pharisees had a problem, for they could not agree that Jesus came from God. We also learn that healing is a personal experience which cannot be denied - try as they might they could not deny the man's experience when he said "one thing I know, that, whereas I was blind, now I see" (v25). We learn that healing involves a personal relationship, or obedience - it was not the paste of dust and saliva that healed him, but his obedience to the command of Jesus. If he had not obeyed, he would not have been healed.

Another lesson we learn from this story comes from the response of Jesus, when asked about whose sin was responsible for the man's blindness. Jesus said nobody sinned, but that the purpose for the blindness was that the works of God might be manifest or revealed. At first glance this statement appears to mean that God designed that this man be born blind so that, at some point in his adult life, he might be healed by Jesus to demonstrate the power of God. In the mean time he had to endure years of visual disability. This meaning is unlikely as it does not fit in with Jesus' teaching about God's love, and concern for people. How then are we to understand what Jesus meant? What he was saying was not that the man was born blind in order that God's power and glory might be made manifest in his healing, but that given that the man was born blind, the result would be that God's power and glory will be manifest in his healing. Jesus denies the cause which the disciples suggested, and turns abruptly from the cause of the blindness to its consequences, namely, the opportunity it provides to glorify God. Furthermore from Jesus' answer to the disciples and Pharisees; we understand that healing demands compassion, not curiosity. It demands action, not discussion (v4). Also physical healing always has spiritual meaning and so sometimes needs to be followed up. That is why Jesus sought out the man after he had been thrown out of the synagogue (v35). Healing should affect our relationship with God (v38). And finally Christian healing always involves challenge (v.39) - a challenge to worship God the Healer and consecrate one's life to him, or to pass by him and remain spiritually blind[42].

CONCLUSION
This chapter concludes with the presentation of two 'timeless' promises by Jesus to all believers. These promises are

discussed below:

Mark 16:17-18

> *And these signs shall follow them that believe; In my name shall they cast out devils; they shall speak with new tongues: They shall take up serpents; and if they drink any deadly thing, it shall not hurt them; they shall lay hands on the sick, and they shall recover.*

The rich cluster of divine promises in this passage hinges on faith. There seems to be no grounds for the attempt of some to limit this promise to apostolic times. This text is addressed to "He that believeth" in every generation and period of the church's history. When Jesus gives the command to the twelve to heal all manner of sickness and all manner of diseases, we may well be right to conclude that this was an apostolic commission, and therefore not applicable to us, but here lies a promise not only to the apostles, but to those who should believe on Christ through the word of these apostles. Whatever practical difficulties we may have in regard to the fulfilment of this word, these ought not to lead us to limit it where the Lord has not. The safe position on this scripture is to assert the perpetuity of the promise, and with the same emphasis, to admit the general weakness and failure of the church to appropriate it by faith. The reason many miracles are now not wrought, is not because the church is already established, but rather because unbelief reigns. Admission of human failure on the part of the church is a far safer and more rational refuge for the Christian, than the implication that God has changed His mind about healing today.

Mark 16:17-18 is the only mention of healing in relation to the final commission of Jesus to his disciples. These verses anticipate that those who believe as a result of the preaching of the gospel will cast out demons, and lay hands on the sick so that they will recover. They are a promise and a prophecy that the apostles and those who believe will do these things as an indication or sign of their faith. This long ending of Mark's gospel can be regarded as authentic because the passage would not have been included in the canon of Scripture unless it was believed to authenticate that experience as what Jesus intended for his disciples[43]. We know from Acts that the disciples continued to heal the sick after Jesus left them at the ascension; which suggests that they understood that it was His intention and desire that they should do so. They would not do what they had no authority to do. They believed the promise in Mark16:17-18 and continued to heal in Jesus name, their example is therefore part of the basis and authority for the church to engage in its ministry of healing today.

John 14:12-13

Verily, verily, I say unto you, He that believeth on me, the works that I do shall he do also; and greater works than these shall he do; because I go unto my Father. And whatsoever ye shall ask in my name, that will I do, that the Father may be glorified in the Son.

It is startling that Christ says we will do the works that He did, but it is stupendous when he declares that those who believe in Him will also do greater works than he did. This unmistakably means whatever miracles he did on earth will be transcended by the miraculous works of those who believe in Him. How is this possible? The answer is given in Jesus' own words - "because I go to the Father". Jesus in heaven will have far greater power and authority than he had in his earthly ministry (Matt 28:18-19), and thereby He will enable those who believe in Him to do greater works than he did[44]. Yet another question may be asked, how does his going "to the Father", and receiving all power and authority bring about greater earthly miracles? The answer is in John 14:16-17. The Holy Spirit would come to make all this possible. Hence when the Spirit of truth, the helper, comes from heaven, the connection between heaven and earth would be made, and believers would do greater works than Christ did when He was on earth. When Jesus was on earth he was restrained geographically, but after the coming of the Holy Spirit there was no longer a geographical restraint. Jesus said it would be to our profit for him to leave, because when he goes the Holy Spirit would come. In summary – not only would miracles and healings continue after Jesus' earthly ministry but they would be even greater. And they would be performed not only by apostles, prophets, and the like, but also by others who would believe in Him through the entire age of the proclamation of the gospel; and this accords well with Mark16:17.

The disciples were promised by Jesus that after his ascension they would be able to do the same works and even greater than He had done while he was with them. These works (Greek - 'erga') of which Jesus speaks include his works of healing, as this word is commonly used of his miracles in the gospels. This promise clearly looks beyond the days of the apostles, and does not set any time limits, nor is it restricted to the apostles. It is an open ended statement. The works referred to would include salvation and all kind of miraculous works. Despite the church's failure to meet up with the promise, it remains true and valid, and cannot be explained away. After this promise Jesus goes on immediately to say "whatever you ask in my name, I will do it, that my Father may be glorified in the Son (John 14:13). This suggests that when the time came to do the same works as he had done, they could request the power to do them through prayer[45]. We can be sure that answer to prayer is not restricted to any dispensation.

The kingdom of God involves restoring everything to its proper order. The Christian is God's representative and ambassador here on earth to enforce His authority. The forces of nature, then, must obey when we pray backed by the authority of God. The kingdom of God is not in word only. We deform the gospel if we choke it with a stream of words without a demonstration of power.

Chapter 8

The Healing Ministry Of The Apostles

Is this the blue print for the church today?

Ms K had fallen from a horse, hurt her back badly and her limbs had been so affected that she became crippled, unable to walk or perform tasks. She had to have someone care for her. One day her carer sat her down in a comfortable chair, and went to the garden. She had not been long in the garden when she heard a rumbling noise in the house. Thinking that the cripple had tumbled out of her chair she rushed inside to find Ms K at the far end of the room praising God, who had made her completely whole! The carer sent for her neighbour who came in haste and was astonished at the sight he saw. All the while Ms K was in ecstasy, taking no notice of the company, but running about the house and, every now and then, falling on her knees to praise God, who had made whole a daughter of Abraham, who had been bowed down for ten or a dozen years. Since the cripple was alone when the miracle happened she had to recount the events by herself. This is what she said: "While I was musing on these words, "Eneas, Jesus Christ maketh thee whole,"(Acts 9:33-35) I could not help breathing out my heart and soul in the following manner: "O that I had been in Eneas's place" Upon that I heard a voice saying, "Arise, take up thy bed and walk!" The suddenness of the voice made me start in my chair; but how astonished was I to find my back strengthening and my limbs recovering their former use in that start! I got up, and to convince myself that it was a reality and not a vision, I lifted up my chair and whatever came in my way; I went to my room and took up my bed, and put my strength to other trials, till I was convinced that the cure was real, and not a dream or delusion." This testimony was recorded and endorsed by an eminent Baptist Minister (Rev. Morgan Edwards of New Jersey)[46].

The only divinely inspired record we have of church life is one in which miracles and supernatural guidance are quite common. The account in Acts is the only period in church history where we can be absolutely certain of God's opinion of church life and ministry. The book of Acts is the best source we have to demonstrate what normal church life should look like. When the Holy Spirit is present and working in the church, we find a church that has passion for God, and is a miracle-working church. Why would anyone think that God would want the church today to be different? Would anyone seriously prefer as a model of normal church life, a church in the time of the reformation or perhaps, a traditional church in twenty-first century modern Britain?

The book of Acts reveals that God performed many miracles in the early church. It is evident that many more healing miracles were performed than are recorded in Acts. In Acts healing appears in the teaching of the apostolic church which recognised that preaching and healing were combined in the earthly ministry of Jesus Acts 10:36-38. What can we learn about healing from the apostles (men of like passion)? We shall now survey some of these healing accounts.

The man at the beautiful gate (Acts3:2-8, 16)

And a certain man lame from his mother's womb was carried, whom they laid daily at the gate of the temple which is called Beautiful, to ask alms of them that entered into the temple; who seeing Peter and John about to go into the temple asked an alms. And Peter, fastening his eyes upon him with John said, Look on us. And he gave heed unto them expecting to receive something of them. Then Peter said, silver and gold have I none; but such as I have give I thee; In the name of Jesus Christ of Nazareth rise up and walk. And he took him by the right hand, and lifted him up: and immediately his feet and ankle bones received strength. And he leaping up stood, and walked and entered with them into the temple, walking, and leaping and praising God.... (v16) ...... through faith in his name hath made this man strong, whom you see and know; yea, the faith which is by him hath given him this perfect soundness in the presence of you all.

The account of the lame man at the beautiful gate reveals that he was healed by word and touch. Peter asked him to fix his attention on them and then ordered him in the name of Jesus Christ of Nazareth to walk. At the same time, he took the man by the right hand and helped him up and as he did so, the man's feet and ankles were made strong and he was healed. We can learn a few lessons from this healing account. It appears that healing came for several reasons;
- as a response to a request (Acts 3:3),
- a response to a cripple's need for healing (Acts 3:2),
- a response to faith (Acts 3:16),
- an opportunity to witness to the people and religious

leaders (3:12-16, 4:16,22,30),
- an authentication of the preaching of the word (4:29)
- and a cause for people to glorify God (3:18, 4:21).

The Father of Publius (Acts 28:8-9)

And it came to pass, that the Father of Publius lay sick of a fever and of a bloody flux: to whom Paul entered in and prayed, and laid hands on him, and healed him. So when this was done, others also, which had diseases in the island, came, and were healed:

After Paul's shipwreck on the island of Malta, Publius, the chief official of the island took them into his home. When Paul found his host's father was sick, and suffering from fever and dysentery, he went in, prayed, and laid hands on him and healed him. This account is of particular interest because healing occurs in the context of prayer. Healing is brought about as a response to prayer. This is relevant to the modern church because if it happened then, there is no reason why it should not happen today in the church. The main agent in the church's ministry of healing of the sick is prayer, and that is still available to all in the church today[47].

Aneneas the paralysed (Acts 9:33-35)

And it came to pass, as Peter passed throughout all quarters, he came down also to the saints which dwelt at Lydda. And there he found a certain man named Aeneas, which had kept his bed eight years, and was sick of the palsy. And Peter said unto him, Aeneas, Jesus Christ maketh thee whole: arise, and make thy bed. And he arose immediately. And all that dwelt at Lydda and Sharon saw him, and turned to the Lord.

Aneneas of Lydda had been paralysed and bed-ridden for

eight years. Peter calls him by name and says to him "Jesus Christ heals you" The statement implies that he knew the name of Jesus Christ and his ability to heal. The verb iaomai (heal) in the statement is in a form of Greek present tense, which gives the meaning that - he is healed at the very moment that Peter is speaking to him[48]. Having told Aneneas that he was healed, Peter orders him to make his bed. Aneneas had been unable to do this for the past eight years, and so his ability to do so now would be a significant demonstration of his cure. Another powerful agent in the church's healing ministry is faith, and this is demonstrated here. Healing is effected in response to the faith of the healer and/or the patient. If such faith is present in the modern church, there is no reason why what happened then cannot happen now, and I dare say it still happens in many sectors of the Christian church.

The cripple at Lystra (Acts 14:8-10)

> *And there sat a certain man at Lystra, impotent in his feet, being a cripple from his mother's womb, who never had walked: The same heard Paul speak: who steadfastly beholding him, and perceiving that he had faith to be healed, Said with a loud voice, stand upright on thy feet. And he leaped and walked.*

This healing occurred through Paul in the town of Lystra. While Paul was preaching this man managed to catch his eye. Paul realised immediately that he had faith to be cured. He simply called out in a loud voice, "stand upright on your feet" and the cripple jumped up and walked. The crowd went wild with amazement, thinking Paul and Barnabas were gods disguised as men (in a sense that is what Christians are). It is interesting to note that the method of healing here was by word alone, as well as the faith of the patient. Similar to what we see in the gospels, the man is commanded to do what his sickness had rendered him incapable of doing. The man's feet were restored to normal structure and function, and for the first time in his life, he was able to stand upright and walk. Several interesting points can be gleaned from this account: the man had probably attended the meetings daily but he had not been healed, however on this particular day his expectation was high. His faith had been built up, and Paul was able to discern by the Spirit that he had faith to be healed (in Pentecostal terminology, his faith made a demand on the anointing). This clearly shows that faith is usually a necessary ingredient for healing. The combination of the man's faith, Paul's ability to discern (an interplay of the gifts of the Spirit e.g. knowledge, faith, miracles etc. may be observed in this case) that the man had faith to be healed, as well as his authoritative declaration of the word, produced healing in this case. This combination is not always necessary to produce results, it appears that for every case there are certain ingredients that will bring the desired healing. However we don't always know what is required for all cases of sickness, which is why we don't always obtain desired results.

THE GIFTS OF THE SPIRIT

In this section we shall discuss additional passages which support the case for healing in the epistles. These verses particularly relate to the workings of the Holy Spirit and His gifts within the church.

1Corinthians 12:4, 8-11

> *Now there are diversities of gifts, but the same Spirit. For to one is given by the Spirit the word of wisdom; to another the word of knowledge by the same Spirit; To another faith by the same Spirit; to another the gift of healing by the same Spirit; To another the working of miracles: to another prophecy: to another discerning of spirits: to another divers kinds of tongues; to another the interpretation of tongues: But all these worketh that*

one and the selfsame Spirit, dividing to every man
severally as he will.

In this passage the gifts of healings are plainly included
among the Spirit's supernatural gifts. Gifts of healings are
stated as part of the Holy Spirit's activity in the church. In
teaching the local Corinthian church Paul applies this gift to
the whole church. The teaching plainly indicated that the gifts
of healing were to be the continuing experience in the church.
These gifts of healing are still meant to be in operation in
today's church. Within the church today, there are people who
possess the gifts of healing. These gifts would not exist unless
the church had a healing ministry in which they could be
exercised. From Paul's own practice in Acts 28:8 and Peter in
Acts 9:40, together with what is described in James 5:13-16, it
appears that the gift was typically used in the context of
prayer. One could infer then that the gift of healing and its
exercise consists essentially of the application of earnest
prayer together with the supernatural endowments of the
members of the Christian community.[49] The key to the
operation of this gift is the enhancement of the Holy Spirit -
He gives or allows these gifts to operate as He wills. It does
not appear that the gift can be operated at the will of man - a
man might have been given the gift, but its exercise and
operation seems to be down to the Holy Spirit. Our task as
believers is to learn to recognise our gifts, and use them for the
common good. For those who think they don't have any gift of
the Spirit, perhaps you haven't discovered it. We all have a
gift that can bring healing to others. Whatever our gifts may
be, we can pray for others who need healing. God is the
healer; our job is to be available channels of God's healing
grace and love. As we apply ourselves our faith and strength
grows and we become more yielded to the Spirit.

1Corinthians 12:27-30

> Now ye are the body of Christ, and members in particular. And God hath set some in the church, first apostles, secondarily prophets, thirdly teachers, after that miracles, then gifts of healings, helps, governments, diversities of tongues. Are all apostles? Are all prophets? Are all teachers? Are all workers of miracles? Have all the gifts of healing? Do all speak with tongues? Do all interpret?

The willingness of God to heal is revealed in that He established gifts of healings and miracles in the church . He made provision for the church to continue the works of Christ and to do greater works. This passage is plainly addressed to the church in all places, not just to the assembly at Corinth. Again we see that the gifts of healing are listed as a part of the Holy Spirit's movement in the church, intended for the benefit of believers everywhere. The healing ministry of the Holy Spirit through chosen human vessels has never been withdrawn. Therefore there is no valid reason why it should not be in operation today among true Christian churches. Healing is a sign by which the people could know that the Holy Spirit is working in them in the here and now.

Gifts of healings are wholly supernatural endowments. They are not natural gifts nor are they the result of developed skill. Gifts of healings, however, may use natural or material means such as human touch (Acts 28:8) or the anointing oil (James 5:14). In summary, natural means may be used; however, there is no suggestion that the natural or material means in themselves had any curative power. The gift of faith is closely related to the gifts of healings, the gift of faith is the background and energising force for the gifts that follow, the most immediate one being gifts of healings. Where the gift of faith is present there is an atmosphere conducive to healings. Matt 17:20 gives a good demonstration of the vital connection between faith and healing. Faith makes possible the healing of even the most desperate condition. Jesus alone is the healer, and only by faith in Him and in His name can a gift of healing be imparted to another. The gifts of faith and healings are closely connected but not the same. The gift of faith makes an impression on all the succeeding gifts; however it is distinct from others.

Romans 8:11

> But if the Spirit of him that raised up Jesus from the dead dwell in you, he that raised up Christ from the dead shall also quicken your mortal bodies by his Spirit that dwelleth in you.

Those who would disallow this text as evidence in favour of divine healing tell us that it refers solely to the future resurrection of the saints, and not to present experience. While it does have that ultimately in view, it also has the present in mind. In this passage Paul states that God raised up Jesus from the dead, he uses the Greek word egeiro, the usual word for raising from the dead. But when he says that God will also quicken your mortal bodies by his Spirit that dwelleth in you, he changes to zoopoieo" which means to infuse life or vitalise. Paul possibly switched verbs to suggest a life-infusing ministry of the Holy Spirit even now while we are still in the mortal body[50]. 1Cor 3:16 says that we are the temple of the Holy Spirit, it should not be surprising therefore, that the Holy Spirit has distinct ministries to the physical bodies of individual Christians. Would He not prefer His human temples in best repair - the outer fabric as well as the inner shrine? The Holy Spirit indwells us and works to help our inner man to conform to Christ in every way; does He not desire a corresponding healthiness for His physical dwelling place? If we truly are honouring the body as the Spirit's temple and are living in affectionate yieldedness to our saviour-king then we can expect the Holy Spirit to exercise His health-renewing ministry in our mortal bodies according to Romans 8:11.

THOSE WHO WERE NOT HEALED

Some theologians have supported their arguments against healing in the present day church by citing examples of those who were not healed. In this section we shall discuss the three "who were not healed" in the New Testament and in the next chapter we shall discuss the case of "Paul's thorn in the flesh":

Epaphroditus (Philippians 2:26-27,)

For he longed after you all, and was full of heaviness, because that ye heard that he had been sick. For indeed he was sick nigh unto death: but God had mercy on him; and not on him only but on me also, lest I should have sorrow upon sorrow.

Epaphroditus was a leader in the church at Philippi, and had brought gifts from that church to cheer Paul in prison in Rome. He contracted an infection from which he nearly died, but he eventually recovered from his illness. The interesting fact for our present discussion is that it seems Paul was unable to heal him, either through the use of the special gift of healing, or by faith or prayer. The disease was allowed to run its course and even to bring him close to death. His eventual recovery is said to be the result of the operation of the natural healing process of his body[51]. There are more insights about healing to be gleaned from the account of Epaphroditus' sickness. We can safely say that Paul must have prayed for his sick companion, but it seems that there was no immediate result. This shows clearly that healing is not always immediate. The case of the blind man of Bethsaida Mark 8:22 demonstrates this. When Jesus touched him the first time, he said he could only see men as trees walking. It was on the second attempt of Jesus that the man saw clearly. The second point to note is that there is no way to prove conclusively that it was not the prayer of Paul and other Christians that eventually brought recovery. There is no way to determine that Paul's prayer did not procure the healing. It is quite possible that he was healed by the body's natural healing ability, but it could be that Paul's prayer enhanced this ability. There is absolutely no way to know how, and what exactly brought about the healing. The fact that Epaphroditus was not healed immediately is therefore not a valid argument for non-healing, nor is it evidence for the theory of gradual cessation of healing in the church. The account teaches us clearly that healing might not always be immediate, and the ways God chooses to heal are varied, and could include the body's natural healing ability.

Timothy (1 Timothy 5:23)

> *Drink no longer water, but use a little wine for thy stomach's sake and thine often infirmities.*

In this account Timothy is advised to take a little wine for the sake of his stomach and frequent sickness. The account seems to suggest that Timothy suffered frequently from some form of illness. It is suggested that wine is mentioned in the medicinal context[52]. Whatever the clinical details of Timothy's illness, it is interesting to note the apparent preference of medical prophylaxis or treatment to charismatic treatment. We are not told the outcome of the treatment, but it appears Timothy served God unhindered after taking this prescription from Paul. The obvious question we are faced with is why was Timothy allowed to suffer frequent infirmities and not healed by someone with the gift of healing, or by the prayer of faith, or even by Paul who had healed many in the past? Another lesson we learn here is that there are some things we will never understand fully here on earth because we know in part. Also we learn that God, or faith in God, is not contradictory to the use of medical means. Healing comes from God and He determines the way or means through which he brings it to us.

Trophimus (2 Timothy 4:20b)

Trophimus have I left at Miletum sick

Trophimus was a travelling companion of Paul on his 3rd missionary journey (Acts 20:4) and was with him in Jerusalem, where he was the cause of Paul's arrest and imprisonment (Acts 21:27-34). Trophimus was a close associate of Paul, and it is therefore all the more surprising that Paul left him behind in Miletum sick 2Tim 4:20. Again the problem arises about why no one was able to secure his healing either through prayer, the gift of the Spirit or by faith. As in the case of Epaphroditus, his recovery seems to be left to the natural bodily process of healing, and neither charismatic nor medical methods were applied[53]. We do not have enough information about Trophimus to determine the outcome of his sickness, but it is likely that he did recover, if he had died of the sickness it is likely this would have been mentioned.

From the above discussion we can see that the experiences of these three are not valid arguments against healing. Amongst the many healed in the New Testament these are the only few exceptions who seem not to have been healed, and from the arguments presented here we may assume they did obtain their healing eventually, though not in the way we would have expected (i.e. immediately as a result of prayer, or the gifts of the Spirit, or the prayer of faith etc.). What is clear from the epistles is that Christian faith and experience does not exempt people from sickness and disease, but when they do fall sick they can be sure that God is in control of the course of the disease, and is willing to restore them to health and grace in His own way.

Chapter 9

Paul's Thorn in the flesh
Was sickness Paul's Thorn in the flesh?

Present day teaching concerning Paul's thorn has sent multitudes, often after many years of terrible suffering, to premature graves, with their course only half run – a constantly recurring and horrible tragedy. The anecdotal story of a minister comes to mind at this point. He had a brilliant and vibrant ministry but when he became seriously ill, he retired and withdrew into the shadows. Another minister who knew him well became concerned about him, and went to see him and enquired about his situation. He told this minister he had been very sick, and as a result, could not continue with his ministry. When the minister suggested they should pray for his healing, the sick minister said there was no need to pray because he had seen a vision of an angel in bright light who said "it is not my will to heal you". He assumed it was the angel of the Lord, so he had retired from ministry. The other minister shared from scripture with him, and he saw that this was not the angel of God, but Satan appearing as an angel of light. Soon after he prayed to God for his healing and was totally healed and restored.

It must be said that no one really knows the identity of Paul's "thorn in the flesh" The expression "thorn in the flesh" is only used as an illustration in both the Old and New Testaments. The symbol of the thorn in the flesh is not in one single instance in the bible used as a symbol of sickness. Every time the expression is used in the entire bible, the exact identity of the thorn in the flesh is specifically stated. In Numbers 33:55 and Joshua 23:13 for example the thorn refers to the inhabitants of Canaan. In 2Sam 23:6 the sons of Belial were likened to thorns. In all these cases thorns are personalities. Paul's thorn is described as a messenger of Satan or Satan's angel. The Greek word angelos appears almost 200 times in the bible. In all cases it is a person and not a thing and certainly never a disease. Paul tells us this satanic messenger angel came "to buffet me". Here buffet means "blow after blow" as when waves beat against a boat. Mark 4:37[54]. I am of the persuasion that Paul's thorn was satanic persecution, and not a disease. The widespread error concerning Paul's thorn in the flesh misrepresents the Gospel, and distorts the foundation upon which faith for healing must rest.

PAUL'S THORN IN THE FLESH (2 CORINTHIANS 12:7-10)

And lest I should be exalted above measure through the abundance of the revelations, there was given to me a thorn in the flesh, the messenger of Satan to buffet me lest I should be exalted above measure. For this thing I besought the Lord trice, that it might depart from me. And he said unto me, My grace is sufficient for thee: for my strength is made perfect in weakness. Most gladly therefore will I rather glory in my infirmities, that the power of Christ may rest upon me. Therefore I take

pleasure in infirmities, in reproaches, in necessities, in
persecutions, in distresses for Christ's sake: for when I
am weak, then am I strong.

Its Identity

As we have said no one really knows what Paul's "thorn in the
flesh" was. However there is no shortage of theories about the
identity of Paul's thorn, and these can be broadly divided into
two groups. There are theories which identify the thorn as
non-physical, and those which identify the thorn as physical,
all claim to be supported by some passage or the other about
Paul's life from the New Testament. Theories of a physical
thorn include identification of the thorn as; stammering,
deafness, bodily injury from physical violence, a painful
disorder, nervous disease, epilepsy or malaria. Theories which
identify the thorn as non-physical include; religious
opposition, mental oppression, spiritual temptation etc.

These are the features of the thorn in so far as we can discover
from 2 Corinthians 12:7-10; it began when Paul was a mature
adult and a Christian; its onset was sudden; it was recurrent;
its character was personal and painful; its effect was
weakening and humiliating. Paul's thorn did not hinder him
from finishing his course for God (2Tim 4:7). Whatever the
identity of the thorn, no conclusion can be final because the
Scriptures are not clear in this regard. The critical issue is to
understand its meaning and significance. It is to the subject of
the significance of the 'thorn in the flesh' that we shall now
turn.

Its Significance

Regardless of the identity of the thorn in the flesh, Paul leaves
us in no doubt about its significance for him and his spiritual
experience. 2Corinthians 12:7-10 has the following to say
about it; it was a given thing, it was a messenger of satan, it
provided a recurrent source of harassment, it was an antidote
to spiritual pride, it provided a subject for prayer, it caused a

change of attitude, and it witnesses to a special relationship. There can be no doubt that the experience of the thorn in the flesh had great significance for the apostle. Paul tells us that what was once a cause of weakness transformed into a source of strength. This paradox of spiritual experience found expression in the words of the Lord to him - "my grace is sufficient for you", or my grace is enough; it's all you need. My strength comes into fullness in your weakness.

Concerning Paul's thorn in the flesh, Evelyn Frost in her PhD thesis[55] argues that Paul's thorn in the flesh has been magnified out of all proportion as an argument for unanswered prayer for healing, as well as the divine source of suffering. She comments that sometimes the answer to prayer for removal of a thorn is not its extraction, but its transformation. She notes that the thorn was 'a messenger of Satan' (not of God) and that God did not give Paul the thorn in the flesh, but what God gave was such perfect strength that Paul should not be overcome by it. Frost notes that to say that God does not always will that man should have a healthy body or mind is as reasonable as for the prodigal son to persist in continuing in rags when back in his father's house. Answer to prayer for healing should not be measured only by alleviation of pain or symptoms but also in terms of an empowerment to make a firmer and richer surrender of the whole life.

The relevance and meaning

So what is the relevance and meaning of Paul's thorn particularly with reference to Christian healing? The fact that Paul did not describe the nature of his thorn in any detail makes his experience all the more relevant and meaningful for us today in any situation of weakness in which we may find ourselves. The first thing we can learn from Paul's experience of the thorn in the flesh (assuming it was a sickness) is that sickness often has a meaning deeper than merely physical and pathological. In this experience of Paul, the veil is temporarily lifted for us, and we are allowed to glimpse something of the context and purpose of human sickness. Also we cannot fail to see that he actually was subject to disease and sickness or persecution like other people (even though he was a strong Christian). At the same time we can see that God is in control, and he has allowed the sickness for a definite purpose. We can thus see that Paul's thorn was not arbitrary, but in God's providence. We cannot but notice the origin of sickness; it was a messenger of Satan, allowed by God but sent by the adversary of God, just as in the case of Job (Job 2:7). If there were no evil in the world there would be no sickness or disease. The thorn in the flesh provides a good illustration of the working of divine providence. The thorn was given by Satan but used by God for a beneficent purpose. Instead of the thorn crippling Paul permanently, it made him realise his weakness and God's sufficient grace; in short it made him more dependent on God. The thorn never got out of God's control and it helped keep Paul from falling into the sin of spiritual pride. Prayer is the natural response of the Christian to sickness, and here Paul gives us an example of how we should pray. His prayer was persistent and specific, aimed at removal of his thorn. We also learn from Paul's experience that a Christian's prayer is never unanswered. Sometimes 'No' is as much an answer to prayer as 'yes'. God was saying 'no' to his request for the removal of the thorn, but a no to the removal of the thorn is not necessarily the same as no to healing. God in his infinite and manifold wisdom and grace had another way he purposed to deal with the problem. He was not going to remove it; he was going to transform it so that the thorn though not removed was transformed from a hindrance to a channel of grace for Paul's benefit. Paul's experience of his thorn in the flesh is not only a lesson in prayer but a lesson in healing.

We see that there is more than one method of healing; this has already become obvious from this study. Paul's healing was not left to the natural healing processes of the body, nor treated by medicine, nor healed by the exercise of the gift of healing, nor by faith, but by the provision of an antidote of grace to counteract the debilitating effect of his thorn in the flesh[56]. Paul's experience of the thorn has significance for today as a source of reassurance and encouragement. We do not usually have the privilege of getting a glimpse of the purpose of our experience of affliction as it was for Paul. However, Paul has recorded his experience for our encouragement so that when affliction or illness comes to us, we can take comfort and be reassured that it has a providential context (in other words God knows about it, he is in control and he has the answer). And that in our experience of weakness, we, like him, can expect to know the strength God's grace in Jesus Christ can provide. This grace working, through the various methods God has provided and revealed to us, will produce healing. In the hour of pain and suffering, Christians can know that their experience is not an accident outside the purpose of God resulting from suspension of his providence, but a situation in which God is very active for good on their behalf.

Assuming that Paul's thorn was sickness, the fact that Paul prayed for his healing at all meant that this was the norm; the fact that he prayed thrice meant that he fully expected to get results. It meant that God had promised it and had healed in response to prayer in the past, and he would continue to do so. It meant that healing was in his will. It was taken for granted that healing would proceed from the request. It just so happened that in this exceptional case God had something else planned, he was going to answer in another way. We can say that though Paul's thorn was not removed, his prayer was answered because the thorn was no longer a problem or "dis – ease" to him because of God's grace released to him. This in itself is one level of healing or wholeness, i.e. when the physical affliction actually ceases to be a problem. The issue of Paul's thorn is therefore not a valid argument for non-healing but actually is a revelation of one of the ways God might act in His answer to our prayer.

Chapter 10

History Repeats Itself

Is there evidence of God's healing power from church history (post-apostolic period)?

Philip Melancthon had fallen gravely ill on a journey, and a messenger was sent to Luther about the situation. When Luther arrived Philip was about to give up the ghost. His eyes were set; his consciousness was almost gone; his speech had failed, and also his hearing; his face had fallen; he did not recognise anyone and he had ceased to take food or drink. When Luther saw him he was filled with utmost dismay. He turned to his fellow travellers and said: "Blessed Lord, how has the devil spoiled me of this instrument!" (i.e. the devil has almost stolen my helper in ministry). Then turning away towards the window he called most devoutly on God. Luther prayed and urged God with all the promises he could repeat from Scripture, and requested that God must hear and answer now if He would ever have the petitioner (i.e. Luther) trust in

Him again. After this he took the hand of Philip, and said to him; be of good courage, Philip, thou shalt not die. While he uttered these things, Philip began to revive and to breathe, and gradually recovered and was restored to health. Melancthon, writing to a friend says: "I should have been a dead man had I not been recalled from death itself by the coming of Luther" and Luther speaks in the same manner, writing to friends: "Philip is very well after such an illness, for it was greater than I had supposed. I found him dead, but, by an evident miracle of God, he lives"[57].

Luther has been quoted as disparaging miracles, signs and wonders because of his violent revolt against the superstitious pseudo-miracles of the corrupt Roman church in his day. In contrast to his opposition to the corrupt ecclesiastical system, the testimony of Luther's prayers for the healing of the body are among the strongest of any on record in modern times. In 1540 after he saw his colleague Philip Melanchthon restored to health through prayer[58], Luther wrote out instructions for an order of service in 1545 for healing based on James 5[59].

While some scholars take it for granted that the power to heal the sick once given to the disciples by their master was endowed to the church in principle,[60] others argue that the power to heal is confined to the ministry of the apostles, and claims to continuation of miracles into the post apostolic period (ca 100-150) are unfounded[61].

Why are we interested in the history of healing in the Christian church? If we can find even a few healing accounts or miracles in the history of the church after the time of the apostles then the whole theory that miracles ceased after the apostolic period falls on its face.

One of the reasons some Christians do not believe in miraculous gifts is that they have not seen miracles, and they feel there is no real evidence of miraculous gifts through out church history after the death of the apostles. This is not a biblical inference but a deduction based on experience. Our deductions must be based on Scripture and not experience. If indeed in the history of the church the miraculous gifts appear to be lost we need to find out why they were missing, since no clear and specific statements of Scripture say that miracles will cease during the church age.

But were the gifts really lost? There is ample evidence throughout church, history for the use of the gifts in the church but this evidence has largely been handled in a biased way, and often the reports of miracles have been discredited because the witnesses were allegedly gullible and the theology was wrong. From the fourth century on, there are numerous eyewitness reports of miracles and these eyewitnesses were outstanding scholars, theologians, preachers, organisers of the age e.g. Jerome, the leading biblical scholar of his day, Gregory of Nyssa, Athanasius, Chrysostom, the greatest preacher of that day, Ambrose, the greatest churchman of his time, as well as Augustine the greatest thinker of his day, strangely all of these leaders are dismissed as unreliable witnesses to miracles[62]. However more recent research in church history is tending to view the reports of miraculous events throughout the history of the church in a much more positive light[63].

There is much historical evidence for the gifts of healings and miracles throughout the history of the church, and a few excerpts from the words of the early church personalities will suffice here.

> Many of our people have healed and still continue to heal in every part of the world and even in your city (Rome)[64]. – (Justin Martyr 100-165)

> Through laying on of hands, maladies were healed, even the dead are raised, who afterward remained alive in the church for many years. Those who are in truth disciples have received grace from Him to perform miracles in His name. According to the gift which each has received from Him, others still heal the sick by laying their hands

upon them and they are made whole[65] – (Irenaeus c. 125 –200)

Many men of rank, and even much more common people, have been delivered from devils and healed of diseases[66]. – (Tertullian c. 160-220).

Some Christians give evidence of having received, through their faith, a marvellous power, by the cures which they perform, invoking no other name over those who need their help than that of God and of Jesus. For we have seen many persons freed, by those means, from grievous calamities and from madness and countless other ills which could not be cured by men[67] (Origen c.185- c.254)

Throughout our whole habitable world there is no country or a nation or a city where these wonders are not commonly spoken of[68]. (Chrysostom 345-407)

The Bishop of Milan records the incident of a blind man being healed through touching the border of the garments in which the bodies of two martyrs were discovered beneath the pavement of the church, and says, "is not this what we read in the gospel?[69] (St. Ambrose A.D. 340-397),

Even a keen critic like Tholuck concedes: Down into the third century we have credible testimonies of the persistence of the miraculous forces which were active in the first century[70] – A. Tholuck.

There are successive evidences of healings and other miracles down to the age of Constantine[71] – Marshal (Translator of Cyprian).

Witnesses who are above suspicion leave no room for doubt that the miraculous powers of the Apostolic age continue to operate at least into the 3rd century[72] – Gerhard Uhlhorn.

"How often has it happened and still does, that devils have been driven out in the name of Christ; also that by calling on his name in prayer the sick have been healed"[73] – Luther

In the healing of maladies which are incurable, such as cancer, consumption, when the patient was in the agonies of death, they were healed all by means of prayer, or of a single word[74]. – The Moravians.

Supernatural gifts were manifested in the church and miraculous cures were wrought[75] - The Scottish covenanters.

Richard Baxter, the most prolific penman of the English Puritans wrote: How many times have I known the prayer of faith to save the sick when all physicians have given up as dead![76] - Richard Baxter

With regard to the continuance of miracles after the apostolic age, we have testimonies not only from Tertullian and Origen, who tell us that many in their time were convinced against their will, of the truths of Christianity by miraculous visions, but also much later, from others who assert that many heathen among us are being healed by Christians from whatever sickness they have, so abundant are miracles in our midst.

Augustine in his early writings claimed that healing had ceased in the church, and was no longer necessary. But experiences in his own life changed his view. Notably, in his own diocese nearly seventy attested miracles took place over a course of two years. In 427, just three years before he died, Augustine, in his book of Retractions, took back what he had said in his early writings (De Vera Religione) about the age of miracles being past, and described miraculous cures which he had seen and which were enough to change his mind[77].

The practice of healing through prayer never died out in the early church and was evident in later centuries; evangelists of the Waldensian church, George Fox (1642-1691)[78], The Quakers, John Wesley (1703-1791), the founder of Methodism[79, 80].

Can the testimony of these early church Fathers as to the continuing prevalence of miracle healing be accepted as honest, well informed and reliable? When we look at their intellectual stature, sobriety, definiteness and unanimity, we believe the answer must be yes. Healing had an integral, accepted and expected role in the early church and this is attested to in the writings of the church fathers. The one vital point that must be noted about these testimonies is their decided concurrence as acknowledged authorities on the subject that such charismata (i.e. supernatural activities of the Holy Spirit) did continue plentifully for so long after the close of the apostolic interval.

The 5th century is usually known as the dark ages because of its intellectual and spiritual stagnation (at least from a Protestant viewpoint). During this time, before the time of the reformation we even have testimonies of continuing healing from the Waldenses, the Monastic orders and those who remained true to the faith. Despite an apostatized church exerting a pseudo-Christian ecclesiastical tyranny, it appears that healing continued where people were true to the faith. St. Cyprian wrote, "the sins of Christians have weakened the power of the church", and though the early church rationalised and pretended that God had "withdrawn the gifts", or no longer "willed to heal," and that Christians had to "bear their sufferings as Christ his cross," and that illness was "a punishment for sin and must not be interfered with", yet the grim truth was sin and decay in the church[81].

Even a great sceptic who asserts that miracles ceased with the passing away of the apostles concedes that "some at least of these (miracles/healing) appear to be supported by evidence sufficient to establish their truth." He also states that there are no limits to the possibilities of faith[82]. And no one can contradict the power of prayer in bringing healing or miracles, or say what God can or cannot do in answer to prayer. Answers to prayer have not passed away, faith still produces the impossible. A few others cessationists sometimes, unwittingly perhaps, puncture their own theories by stray admissions[83].

Therefore, from the unimpeachable testimony of the early church Fathers, corroborated by collateral evidences such as we have quoted, and which have been accepted by many scholars of later times as being trustworthy[84], I present my case that healing and miracles continued well after the apostolic days until now, though with intermissions for various reasons, - mainly the condition of the professing church. This seems the truest position to the evidence. Multitudes have been healed since the days of the apostles, down to and including our days in particular, it is to these we shall now turn.

Chapter 11

The Testimony Of The Healed
Does God still heal today?

I have to admit that one of the most convincing arguments is always that based on experience. Jesus said

> *"Go back and tell John what you have seen and heard: the blind see again, the lame walk.....and blessed is the man who does not loose faith in me". (Lk 7:22-23 paraphrased).*

In this chapter we will answer the question; "is there attested evidence today that God is still healing by prayer, spiritual gifts or miracles"? We will examine some present day testimonies of healing which are believed to be true, well attested and corroborated. The testimonies are from a range of credible documented sources from the 19th century to present day. These testimonies are designed to inspire you and build your faith in God's healing power and compassionate love.

They are also designed to show you that God's healing power is available today to those who come to Him. In my own local church, (Glory House London) healing and miracles are a common occurrence, some of which have been well documented[85].

In reporting these testimonies one could be regarded as very simple minded, nevertheless simplicity is one of the soft and formative stages of all true faith. The first announcements of the resurrection were deemed as "idle tales" by those who heard them; and had it not been for the credulity of the simple-minded women who first reported this miracle, we might not have had the faith of the strong-minded men like Peter, who afterwards preached it. The testimonies are presented in the ensuing subsections. As you read these testimonies I pray your faith will be emboldened and strengthened.

The Woman in a Coma[86]

The Doctors called it a medical miracle; the news paper front page read "Woman Awake, Alive, Healthy After Two Years in Coma". A minister had been asked to pray for this lady, he had no idea how seriously ill she was. The doctors had said she had no hope for living and if she ever regained consciousness would basically be a vegetable because she had extensive brain damage. Over the course of one year which involved more than 60 hospital visits, she was healed, through consistent and persistent prayer. The week in which she was healed her condition had become worse and it seemed that she would probably die. The minister testified that he had turned to God many times throughout the course of that year asking God if He had really sent him to that girl. Each time God gave him the assurance: "I sent you. Don't quit". His persistence was rewarded when after two years in hospital; she woke up with full restoration to her brain. Every hour and every tear that had been invested became worth the wait when she woke up and gave glory to God.

Healed of Cancer[87]

This is the testimony of a Baptist Policeman from Houston Texas who was healed at Kathryn Kuhlman's healing Crusade. Verified and attested to by Physicians. Kathryn Kuhlman was one of the most well known and phenomenal healing evangelists of her time. The Policeman, who we'll call Captain LV had been a veteran of 33 years on the police force. Following a routine physical examination and a subsequent visit to the specialist he was told he had cancer. The cancer was malignant and advanced so they referred him to specialist doctors from the tumour institute. They offered him radiation treatment, not much hope and about a year to live. Captain LV remembered that in his church they prayed for the sick every Wednesday night, he believed that God was able to heal, but he assumed that God wasn't in the miracle-performing business today. So when he went for radiation treatment the only prayer he knew to say was "Lord, let this machine do what it was designed to do".

After about four months he was in severe pain and was taken to the hospital again, they found that the cancer had had eaten a hole all the way through his hip, only the outer skin was covering the cavity. His radiation treatment began again, he kept on working as a police officer but was growing weaker everyday. The doctors recommended surgery but before he was due for surgery the cancer appeared again in his spine and the pain more excruciating than ever imaginable. It was only a matter of time before death. He went on what was supposed to be his last holiday with his family, then one day in early fall he turned on the TV to watch a program called "Higher Ground" hosted by his church. As the program ended he heard a lady's voice on the TV say *"I believe in miracles"*, he glanced up, he was not very impressed by the woman preacher he was a Baptist, but as the program progressed and this woman talked about wonderful healing miracles something inside him clicked, *"can this be for real?"* he wondered. The show closed and he saw a name of a friend on the screen so he called his friend and asked if the healings were real, his friend confirmed that they were. He told his friend he had cancer, his friend sent him Miss Kuhlman's books. He made arrangements to go for her meeting, he knew his time was running out.

On February 19 of that year he flew from Houston to Los Angeles for the meeting. Captain LV recounts that when the doors opened the people came pouring down the isles like lava down the sides of a volcano. When he saw all the sick people, in wheel chairs some so twisted and some so disfigured, he wanted to cry. He felt so selfish, he prayed "Oh Lord, am I selfish wanting a healing when there are so many people here, some so young?" Then he heard God's voice in his heart saying, "There is no shortage in my storehouse".

He made his way up the isle and found a seat in the first row of the balcony. When the service started there was singing and sharing of testimonies. The atmosphere was different, maybe it was the sense of expectancy or awe but Captain LV says whatever it was, this was different from any other meeting he had ever attended. Then Miss Kuhlman began to speak "I believe in Miracles. I believe that You're healing today like You were when Jesus Christ was here. You know the need of the people here, all over this huge auditorium. I pray that you will touch them. In the name of Jesus I ask it. Amen." Then there was silence and suddenly she started speaking rapidly as she received the word of knowledge about people's situations. Miracles and healings started happening all over the auditorium it was phenomenal and amazing people were crying others were praising God. Suddenly she pointed at the left balcony exactly where Captain LV was sitting. "You have come a long way for your healing for cancer, God has healed you. Stand up in the name of Jesus and claim it" Captain LV hesitated and thought how do I know this is for me? Instantly he heard the same inner voice he heard earlier say "stand up". He stood up in faith and in obedience not feeling a thing. As he stood up then it hit him, it was like being baptised in liquid energy, he had never felt such strength flowing through his body. A woman asked if he had been healed of something he said yes and he was told to run up front and testify.

Moments later he was up stage with Miss Kuhlman, she walked to him and just said "we thank you blessed Father for healing this body, fill him with the Holy Ghost" and he fell to the floor under the power, he fell to the floor several times because there was such a surge of power around him. Several people came up stage, mothers with children healed of various maladies. The devil attacked his mind "what makes you think you have been healed" but he knew he was healed, he needed no proof he was sure of it. After the meeting he called his wife and told her, he was sobbing "I have been healed". Even without medical examination he knew he had been healed.

The first doctor to see him was the one who performed the surgery. He gave her a copy of Miss Kuhlman's book "I believe in Miracles". She looked at the book, listened to his story then looked at him like he was nuts. She said to him "Let me tell you something, the only miracle that has happened to you is a medical miracle. That's all. The only thing keeping you alive is your medication. You quit taking it and see how long you'll live." Captain LV smiled and said "well, I haven't had any medication for about a month now" The doctor was shocked and angry and told him it won't be long before the cancer breaks out in another place. Captain LV went to see another of his doctors but decided not to say anything about the miracle and allow him to find out for himself. When the doctor commented on his high spirits he could not resist telling him the story. The doctor said "now look, I'm a Christian too, but God has given us enough sense to look after ourselves". That's the reason why I'm here said Captain LV, but you won't find anything wrong. The Doctor gave him the most thorough physical examination he had ever had, at each stage the Doctor kept repeating "remarkable, remarkable". Even his varicose veins had been healed. The results from the X-ray a few days later showed he was completely healed, no trace of cancer was found.

Cancer Healed[88]

This story was told by a clergy man, about a surgeon friend who operated on the sick woman and found cancer of the stomach too far advanced for further surgical treatment. The woman was sent home to die because the surgeon thought she would not live more than two weeks. Her friends, however, met together regularly to pray for her recovery. Seven years later she was completely well. The surgeon himself said that the only explanation he could give was that she was healed in answer to prayer.

Tubercular disease Healed[89]

This testimony is from Dr Howard Somervell a fellow of the royal College of surgeons and a member of the Mount Everest Expedition in the early nineties. He is unlikely to offer a highly-coloured story of the effect of prayer. He tells the story of a schoolmaster with tubercular disease: "The disease is one which medical science reckons to be well-nigh incurable (at the time) when it has reached this stage. The man was going down hill and daily getting weaker and more feverish. His legs became more and more painful; and after a few weeks we took another X-ray picture and found the disease was worse, in that the whole bone was involved. There was only one thing to do, and that was to amputate the leg to save the patient's life"

Dr Somervell sent copies of the radiograph he had taken to one he regarded as the greatest authority on bone disease in the region. It was confirmed that the disease was tubercular, and the only chance of saving the man's life was to take off his leg at the knee. So he told the poor fellow that there was nothing else to be done. The man's reply was unexpected: "Will you give me three weeks? I want to try the effect of praying about it" It was agreed that he could have that time, so he went home. In three weeks he returned as promised. He had left the hospital feverish, ill, flushed in the face, and only capable of being carried about. He returned in a car, but hobbling with a stick and looking much better. The wound had not healed, but the leg itself, as revealed by the X-Rays, was wonderfully improved, though not totally free from the disease. The Doctors were amazed and asked what he had done to make such great improvement. He told them that he was quite sure it was against God's will for any of his servants to suffer with disease and he knew he still had before him a life of service to God if only he could keep his leg and his life. So he called his family and asked them to join him in prayer and agree with him that he would be completely healed. They agreed and kept up a continuous prayer chain, week after week this continued. When he came to see the doctors again in another three weeks the leg had healed and after a few months he was back at school, perfectly fit, playing games with the boys, running about on both legs with no sign of disease.

Fibroid Tumour Healed[90]

Mrs Carter the wife of a policeman of Spokane, Washington was pronounced by her physicians to be pregnant, after nine months, no child was born, so the doctors gathered and re-examined her, this time they discovered that it was a fibroid tumour . The tumour continued to grow until the 14th month had passed and the doctors estimated it would be about 15 pounds. One day she went to the famous John G. Lake prayer rooms at about 4.00pm with her nurse. She was prayed for and she returned home. By 10am the next morning when she woke there was no more tumour in her, it had totally vanished. There was neither part nor particle of the tumour left, no blood, no pus, and no evidence whatsoever. The tumour totally dematerialised by the power of God.

There are many more testimonies to share but space will not permit to talk about them all; for instance a nurse and her three children all healed of Myasthenia Gravis (an electrical breakdown in the nervous system of the body) in one night at a Kathryn Kuhlman's service[91, 92]. But these should suffice for now.

The actual experience of seeing a crippled man healed (Acts 4:13-17) confronted the religious leaders in the time of Acts with two decisions to make; first a theoretical one – was the healing real or not? And secondly a practical one – what should they do about it? They judged that it was real. But, as for doing something, they decided to forbid it, because they felt it was doctrinally unsound (being associated with preaching the resurrection of Jesus), and would undermine their authority especially since it was done by lay and uneducated men. Today we all, (including the religious leaders) are being confronted by the witnessing to healing that people – many of them "uneducated laymen" – claim to have experienced. Consequently we simply cannot merely discuss healing as a theory but we need to make a judgement: is it true? And if it is, what must we do about it?

Chapter 12

The Power Of Faith & Prayer
Do our prayers really make a difference?

Mrs CS had an ovarian cyst the size of a large egg which resulted in a persistent pain in her abdomen. The doctor said surgery would be necessary to take it out. Mrs CS and her husband asked if they could have some time to get rid of the cyst through prayer. The doctor said they could have two months since he was sure the cyst was not malignant or life threatening. All manner of prayer was prayed to get rid of the cyst; such as prayer of agreement, speaking the scriptures, binding, loosing and casting out etc. Also laying on of hands and anointing with oil was done. No change occurred. Her husband felt he would have to persevere in prayer and obtain the answer through persistent faith, because this is the way most answers to prayer come – not as instant miracles. But by fighting the fight of faith and patience. He felt led by the Spirit to pray for an hour a day for his wife. He thanked God for healing his wife cited the scriptures he was standing on and prayed in the Spirit (in tongues) most of the time. This went on for a month. One afternoon as he was praying in the Spirit, he saw himself holding this cyst in his hand and squeezing the life out of it. He asked his wife if there was any change in the way she felt and she confirmed the pain was decreasing. The doctors said if the pain was decreasing that meant the cyst was shrinking. As he kept on in his daily prayer he kept on seeing (in the spirit) the cyst get smaller and smaller and at a point while he was praying he saw the cyst vanish in his hand. He knew that God was showing him the cyst was gone. After that point he stopped praying and three days later his wife confirmed that the pain had totally gone. Subsequent ultrasounds confirmed what they knew in their hearts – no more cyst![93]

For centuries, families and individuals facing ill health have instinctively made prayer the bedrock of their experience. In the process of healing, it seems a life-sustaining; life creating force reveals itself which is to its core inexplicable. Even high-tech medicine depends on this healing power (which some refer to as God, Nature, or a Higher power) for the success or failure of sophisticated medical treatment, this is the reason for the religious dimension of healing.

When we begin to discuss prayer and its role in healing, we step into a mine field of tough questions, doctrinal differences, and potentially explosive arguments. If God is sovereign and he accomplishes what he wants, when he wants, why pray? Why must we be persistent? How can I pray the prayer of faith for healing, do I ask him just once in faith or do I have to keep asking again and again. Why must we war against the devil if he has been defeated and we have authority as Christians? Is sickness allowed by God or is there something I can do to prevent it. Why does it often take long to get a prayer answered, does God have an appointed time to answer my prayer or does the timing depend on the fervency of my prayers?[94]

Either God wants people healed or He doesn't. If He wants them healed, which is certainly the case, then we must take it for granted (based on the multitude of sick people in our world) that He is either incapable of doing anything about them, or He desires to use us and is waiting on us to be the channels through whom he will bring about healing. If God is going to heal whether we pray or we don't pray, then why pray? We don't need to waste another minute praying for the sick. If it's all que sera, sera, whatever will be will be, then let's take a break, (have a kit kat) and let it all happen.

For many, prayer for the healing of the sick is a hit-or-miss-in-the-dark procedure. Praying for the healing of others seems to threaten us because we fear loosing faith and loosing face if it doesn't "work". Underneath our misgivings about healing prayer lurk the fearful questions, "what if we pray and nothing happens, do such things still happen today?" Others secretly fear that God's promises are just fantasy, a figment of their imagination; God either does not want to heal us or has no power to do so. Better to stay comfortably ignorant and just go through the motions, praying in eloquent generalities, so you can never tell if your prayer is answered or not. This fearful reasoning assumes that we have no role in God's healing process.

In this chapter we will attempt to answer the questions raised. Prayer is critical to the subject at hand and it is an activity in which all must be engaged. Prayer is striking the winning blow, it is a means of harnessing divine energy, there is an atmosphere in which healing is much easier, and this atmosphere may be created by prayer. Prayer for healing brings into play forces far beyond what our own unaided humanity contributes. From the earlier chapters we can see that prayer plays an important role in bringing healing to the sick. We know that Jesus spent long periods in prayer (Mark 1:35). When the disciples enquired why they could not heal the lunatic boy, Jesus answered; "because of your unbelief... however this kind can come out only through prayer" Matt

17:19-21, Mark 9:28-29. We also know that the disciples employed prayer as a means of healing (Acts 28:8, 9:40). James 5:14-16, the classical healing text is unambiguous about the role of prayer in healing and we will examine this text further in the next section.

The Prayer of Faith

James 5:14-16 is the boldest, most explicit pronouncement anywhere in the New Testament on the subject of bodily healing for Christians. It is the biblical cornerstone of the healing ministry for the church. It incorporates prayer, the laying on of hands, anointing and forgiveness of sins.

James 5:14-16

> *Is any sick among you? Let him call for the elders of the church; and let them pray over him, anointing him with oil in the name of the Lord: And the prayer of faith shall save the sick, and the Lord shall raise him up; and if he have committed sins they shall be forgiven him. Confess your faults one to another, and pray one for another, that ye may be healed. The effectual fervent prayer of a righteous man availeth much.*

We observe in James 5:14-16 that the promise of healing is explicit and unconditional "the prayer of faith shall save the sick, and the Lord shall raise him up; and if he have committed sins they shall be forgiven him". James shows that prayer for healing is not for a privileged few or those of superior faith but available to all children of God. The promise is definite; there is nothing doubtful about this prayer, it does not say "the prayer of faith may save the sick" And it does not say "the prayer of faith will save the sick if it is the will of God" (as some scholars insist). The text is addressed originally to any sick person, not to those who have discerned by some special wisdom that they are among the few that God has chosen to heal. Why would the text call for "any" sick, only to narrow down the blessings of healing to a chosen few? If ever a statement was definite James 5:15 is. The promise is inclusive. It excludes none that are truly Christian believers.

The anointing with oil does not refer to the use of medicine (as some scholars suggest) but is symbolic of the Holy Spirit. The use of oil was carried on by the early church until the 18th century, but with time the experience and expectation of healing by this means dwindled. In the early post-apostolic years, the bishop would lay hands upon the patient and anoint him with oil, *if* the elders were men of God who regarded the use of oil as the outward sign of the inward grace and power of God, *if* they had the love of God in their hearts and could convey it to the patient, and *if* the quality of their lives could call forth expectant trust from the patient, healing often followed. But the *"Ifs"* above were rarely fulfilled, and a process that brought no cure could not last indefinitely as a mere ceremonial. Finding that the anointing with oil, had fewer and fewer successes as far as restoration of health was concerned, the very meaning of the service of anointing with oil was subtly altered by the church.

Dr Weatherhead states that the council of Trent in 1549 taught that unction (anointing) "blots out sins, if any remain to be expiated", and strengthens the soul of the patient to bear more easily "the troubles and sufferings of disease..." This is a very different emphasis, and shows the diminished expectation and loss of power which resulted in loss of confidence and faith in the church and her ministers. The emphasis was shifted from healing to forgiveness, but the true emphasis in the early days was on healing. The word "save" in the passage from James 5 means "to make whole" this is the same Greek word used in the story of the woman with a haemorrhage, "Thy faith hath made thee whole" And the word "raise up", in the James 5 passage is the same as that used in the miracle described in Matt 9:5 where Jesus said "arise and walk". Weatherhead concludes that the early Scriptural value of anointing and its main intention in the early church was the healing of the body, but this became difficult because the faith of the church was at a low ebb, the meaning of unction slowly changed, and was relevant almost entirely to the forgiveness of sins.

Nowadays it is used as a rite for the final pardon of the dying. Instead of praying the prayer of faith that heals the sick, they pray that the sick will have fortitude and patience to bear their afflictions[95]. Thankfully Pope Paul VI changed the 'extreme unction' (a service for the final pardon of the dying) to the 'anointing of the sick' (a service for the healing of the sick) bringing the sacrament back in line with the true meaning of James 5:15. The essential form of the sacrament now emphasises healing, whereas the previous emphasised forgiveness of sin this change was effected in the second Vatican council constitution on Liturgy, No. 73[96].

So what is the prayer of faith? First we will agree that it is prayer which is effective in bringing results. From the example of Elijah cited in James 5:17-18 (c.f. 1Kings 18:42-44), Elijah prayed earnestly that it would not rain; he remained in a posture of prayer, he 'prayed with prayer' until the prayer was answered. The prayer of faith in this context is therefore earnest and fervent prayer. While teaching on the subject of prayer Jesus draws a parallel between persistence and faith in the context of the parable of the widow and the unjust judge (Luke 18:1-8). The parable of the friend at midnight is told by Jesus when his disciples asked him to teach them to pray, again he emphasised persistence in prayer (Luke 11:1-13, 21:36). The tense used for "to pray or prayer" in this passage and the passages below is the present infinitive – it refers to continuous or repeated action. The present imperative is also used; this is a command to do something in the future and involves continuous and repeated action[97]. When the disciples asked Jesus to teach them to pray what they were saying was 'teach us to pray continually'.

Other passages emphasising persistence in prayer include Rom. 12:12 ("continuing instant in prayer"), Eph. 6:18 ("Praying always....with all perseverance...."), Col. 4:2 ("Continue in prayer.....")1Thess 5:17 ("Pray without ceasing") hence the prayer of faith could be defined as persevering prayer. To be sure it is not our long prayers, but our faith in God that gets the answer however there are cases when the answer is delayed, our perseverance demonstrates our faith until the answer manifests physically. The prayer of faith is one without wavering, double mindedness or doubt (James 1:5). It is persevering prayer upheld by confident trust in God and His promises. God meets us at our faith level; the centurion, the woman with the bloody issue, Jarius the synagogue ruler. These all obtained their desired healing according to their faith level. If you have a lively belief in God's goodness, and faith that He is on the side of life and health and that He also has the power to bring us healing, then you have the kind of faith that is sufficient to bring about healing.

The Necessity of Prayer

John Wesley said 'God does nothing except by the prayer of the saints'. God chose to work on earth through humans, not independent of them. From the creation of man to the present day, man is God's link to authority and activity on earth. Though God is sovereign and all powerful, He has limited Himself, concerning the affairs of the earth, to work through man-kind. And this is the very reason why the world is in a mess today. This view is supported by Scripture; God says we should pray 'thy kingdom come thy will be done' (Matt 6:10). Surely He would not ask us to pray in this way if things were as He wanted them to be or if His will would be done irrespective of our prayers. The fact is that God's will is yet to be fulfilled on earth. Disease, evil, sin, famine, wars and calamity is not God's will. To establish God's will on earth, we have to make the inroad through our intercessory prayer (Isaiah 62:1 -12).

If God commands us to pray that His will be done on earth according to Matt 6:10, then it follows logically that God's will shall be done on earth only if we pray. The following passages should drive home this point. 1Kings 18 is the account of Elijah praying for rain to end the drought he had prayed for three years earlier. James 5:17-18 states clearly that it was the effectual fervent prayer of a righteous man that stopped the rain and later brought the rain. God said in verse 1 of 1 Kings 18 that He would send rain. So we can see that it was in God's will and timing to end the drought and send rain, yet He required the earnest prayer of a man to bring the rain.

Daniel 9,10 is the account of Daniel's prayer in Babylon. Daniel had discovered from the reading of books a prophecy by Jeremiah (Jer. 29) that the time for the end of the captivity of the Israelites in Babylon had come. One would have thought that it was time to rejoice because the time of restoration had finally come, but instead Daniel went into mourning (fasting, sackcloth and ashes); supplication and intercessory prayer. He continued in prayer until the visitation by the angel Gabriel who revealed to him the intensity of the warfare in the 'heavenlies' (Dan. 10:12). Daniel's persistent prayer helped to secure the 'breakthrough'. It is unlikely that Daniel would have engaged in intercession with fasting if it was not evident to him that prayer had a part to play in bringing the prophecy to pass. It is likely that when the time for the end of the captivity came, God began to seek for a man to lay the burden of prayer on as in Ezekiel 22:30, thankfully He found Daniel and so restoration and deliverance came. From this example we see again that God collaborates with a man to accomplish His own will.

When we examine Ezekiel 22:30-31 we see the result of God limiting Himself to infallible human beings. In this passage God looked for a man to intercede on behalf of the land, finding none, God's indignation and wrath was poured out because His righteousness demanded that sin and rebellion be punished unless there was an intercessor to stand in the gap. The state of the world today painfully tells the same story. Based on the passages discussed above we can only come to the conclusion that with respect to sickness and disease God needs and is waiting on us to bring about the change. God has made the fulfilment of His will dependent on the actions and attitudes of human beings. What an incredible responsibility God has placed on the shoulder of man but what an awesome privilege too.

Persistence in Prayer

A pivotal key to obtaining results in prayer is persistence. Persistence is inseparably connected to faith, true faith will enable you to persevere in prayer. It is through faith and patience (persistent doggedness) that we inherit the promises. Faith and patience have been described as the 'Power twins', indeed they are. Perseverance in prayer is well attested to in Scriptures; Jesus prayed three hours in Gethsemane, Elijah prayed three times before the widow's son was raised (1Kings 17:21), he laboured in prayer 'seven times' (1Kings 18:42-44) before the rains came.

Daniel prayed and fasted for 21 days before he got his answer even though God sent the angel from the first day he started praying. It is interesting that Daniel's prayer was what instigated the sending out of the angel from heaven, therefore it is likely that it was his incessant prayer that released the angel to breakthrough the demonic resistance. If they were praying for what God wanted and it was in God's timing, why did they have to pray persistently before the answer came? Is God hard of hearing or is He limited in power? Surely the answer is a resounding no! God is not limited, He is all powerful but once again we see that He has chosen to limit Himself to working through man whom He has given dominion in the earth.

Another reason why we have to persevere in prayer is because of demonic resistance as we see in the case of Daniel. Our warfare is not with flesh and blood but with principalities, powers and malevolent spirits in high places (Eph. 6:12) who have set themselves against all that is good and godly. Thus our prayers do more than just petition the Father, they actually release increasing quantities of God's power until enough has been released to accomplish His will. We are not talking about vain repetition or asking God again and again as if we were trying to change His mind or badgering the gates of heaven to get to a reluctant Deity. Every time we intercede in prayer a measurable amount of his power is released until we get the break through. In prayer, success goes to the persistent, not to the emotional, eloquent or to the fiery, a tenacious unwavering endurance is often the key to victory in prayer. Prayer, I have learnt is more like a marathon than a hundred meter dash; consistency is the key.

Strong Desire

Desire is a powerful thing, the woman with the issue of blood (Matt 9:20-22) had a strong desire, a 'desperate faith'. One of the reasons why some do not receive the healing they seek is because they are not desperate enough; they want to be healed but don't really have a strong desire for it. When you reach out to God in prayer with all the spiritual energy of your innermost being. There comes into existence, by the creative power of faith that which your soul calls for. That is the reward of focus and a strong desire toward God. When your spirit man is focused on a desire, the forces of life mix with that strong desire, and as that desire intensifies every day, the effect is that the Spirit of God brings to your soul all the elements necessary to create and fulfil the desire of your heart, and one morning the soul awakens to discover that it has become the possessor of the desired object. The prayer of the heart reaches God in an instant. Nobody ever knelt down and prayed sincerely to God that did not instantly touch God. If we had an instrument sensitive and precise enough we might be able to detect the spiritual transmission going on when we pray[98].

The Role of the Holy Spirit

Those who know me well know that Romans 8:26 is one of my favourite prayer Scriptures. This is because I have come to realise that when it comes to prayer, on our own, we are not only limited in strength, but we have inadequate knowledge. Too often we do not know how to pray as we ought. But the Holy Spirit the Parakletos (Gk), i.e. one called (kaleo) alongside (para) us, in order to aid us[99] takes hold together with us against our infirmities and provides the help we need. We involve Him by praying in the spirit, which is actually allowing Him to pray through us. He is omniscient and omnipotent. He knows what and how to pray precisely in every situation and He has the ability to produce results. When we learn to acknowledge and depend totally on Him in our praying He will help our infirmity (weakness) and inability to produce results by adding His strength to ours, thus amplifying the power of our prayer, so we can truly say 'not by might, not by power, but by the Spirit'.

Romans 8:26-27

> *Likewise the Spirit helps us in our weakness; for we do not know how to pray as we ought but that very Spirit intercedes with sighs too deep for words. And God who searches the heart, knows what is the mind of the Spirit, because the Spirit intercedes for the saints according to the will of God. (NRSV)*

There is a seemingly insignificant word in verse 26, it is the word 'ought' some other translations use the word 'should'. In the Greek, 'ought' or 'should' is a legal term which means 'that which is necessary, right or proper in any particular circumstance'[100] thus verse 26 is saying 'we do not know how we must pray or what is necessary to pray in any particular situation in order to produce results. There is 'a how', 'a what' and an ability needed to push through in every prayer situation and the Person who can help us 'pray through' is the Holy Spirit. Sometimes we know what to pray but we don't really know how to pray. Many times we know what and how to pray but we lack the ability to push through in prayer, we sense that something needs to move but we recognise that the ability is wanting. In our prayer for healing this is so relevant, we see the symptoms or perhaps know the diagnosis but we lack the knowledge and/or ability to pray effectively. Dutch sheets in his excellent book 'Intercessory Prayer' sheds interesting light on the role of the Holy Spirit in intercession. He explains the Greek word 'paga' (intercession) with a depth of insight that excites me. Paga, which is the Greek word for intercession has various other, connotations, undertones, and implications. Paga can mean to impinge, to meet or encounter (Gen. 32:1), it can mean setting up boundaries of protection (Joshua 19), it can mean having someone's burden or weakness laid on you, it can imply to light upon (Genesis 28:11). Paga also implies to push against, to strike, attack or to make hostile collision (1Sam.22:18). Intercession brings individuals into contact with God and that is the very meaning of the word to intercede.

The prayer of a committed intercessor will create a meeting either with God or with hostile forces. When the meeting is over, something will have changed. The result might be immediately obvious but sometimes it takes days, weeks or months to observe the fruit of intercession. However when we intercede, cooperating with the Holy Spirit, He is released to go out from us and hover over the situation, releasing His life-birthing energies until that which we are asking comes to pass. By praying in tongues you turn the prayer over to the Holy Spirit who understands, far better than you, what is best to pray for. The prayer, then rises above the limitations of your understanding of the situation.

Generating Power

Prayer generates power and that power can be quantified. Prayer power is real, though we cannot see it; increasing quantities of it exist in the spirit realm. A certain amount of this power or divine force must be released in the spirit realm to accomplish certain things. Different amounts are required for different things. Just like you need different amounts of physical energy for various tasks. The energy you need to lift up this book compared to the amount of power you need to lift up a carton of bricks differ greatly. The same is true for healing. Different amounts of God's power released through prayer is needed to bring about healing for various illnesses. The example that comes to mind is found in Matt 17:14-21, a demon possessed boy was brought to the disciples, the disciples were unable to cast out the demon and so the case was referred to Jesus by the father of the boy. Jesus proceeds to cast out the demon straight away (Jesus proved God's will by healing the boy who could previously not be healed even by his very own disciples). When the disciples asked why they could not cast out the spirit, Jesus tells them it is because of their unbelief and inadequate prayer power (this kind must be cast out by prayer with fasting). Jesus did not have success because He was the Son of God, he did not immediately call for a prayer meeting before He could heal the boy, he had success because he had sufficient (residual) 'prayer power' already generated in his own prayer times (Mk 1:35, Lk 6:12). The disciples had been successful in prior cases of exorcism and healing, hence the implication of this case is that a greater amount of power was required for this particular case and the disciples just did not have it. I am fully convinced that this is one of the reasons why it takes time to get most prayers answered and why we are plagued with the perplexing experience of unanswered prayer. Some people don't have any residual prayer power stored up before hand, others give up on prayer when the answer is delayed, thinking erroneously that delay is denial and so leave God with a half full 'prayer vessel' while God needs a full measure before it can be used to release the desired result.

Praying is much more than asking God for what we desire, it also involves releasing enough power in the spirit to get the job done. Most Christians are not aware of this, after asking, we tend to sit back and wait on God, while He is waiting on us. Sometimes when it appears that God has finally gotten round to giving us what we want, the truth may be that we have finally generated enough prayer power to make it happen. This is not to say that God will not from time to time bless us, and in His mercy bestow His gifts on us even when we have not made adequate power available, however my observation is that God operates by these principles. It would appear then that our unanswered prayer is not necessarily because it is not God's will or timing or even because we lack faith but sometimes because of insufficient 'prayer power'[101].

Spiritual Warfare

When a lesser power meets with a higher, the lesser has to bow and make an exit. About ten years ago I went with some ministers to pray for a mentally sick (demon possessed) man. His sister was a member of my local church and she had asked for prayer for her brother. I decided to go along with the ministers. What we encountered that night was not what I was expecting. As soon as we arrived at the house we heard what sounded like the ravings of a mad man, the man screamed from the upstairs window, he was enraged, it seemed that he or at least the demons in him knew we were coming even before we arrived. He shouted incantations and curses at us and threatened to do us harm. Three of us (including the sister of this man) stood a safe distance away, while two ministers went forward to the door of the house. From where we were standing (shaken but not scared) we started to pray in the spirit. The man ran down stairs threatening. Before he appeared at the door all kinds of images of knife wielding, demon possessed mad men from years of watching unsuitable horror movies and thrillers flashed through my mind. When he opened the door, I prepared for the worst and intensified my prayer. The man stood in the doorway still shouting at the top of his voice, by now the whole street was awake, we could tell from lights coming on in various houses as this happened in the night.

The pastor spoke softly to the man while commanding the foul spirit(s) in him to come out of him. He began to manifest physically turning violent but the pastor remained calm and kept on speaking to the man while casting out the demon. He spat at the pastor, but the pastor was not distracted. He maintained his cool and remained in control. Suddenly the man threw a punch at the other minister, there was a bit of scuffle but it quickly died down, then the man calmed down and seemed to return to his senses. Without any physical restraint or manipulation, the possessed man was totally subdued. Talk about spiritual power. You better believe it, the anointing and power of God is real, and this power can be at work in and through your life also. Shortly after, the police arrived; the neighbours must have alerted them. We assured the police that everything was under control. Soon after this incident this man began to attend church, he was a fine gentleman with a peaceful disposition; he had been delivered by the power of God.

A lesser power met with a higher power, the lesser had to bow and make an exit. Satan is an outlaw, he knows he has been defeated but if we don't enforce his defeat and put him in his place, he will run riot in our lives. Policemen are law enforcement officers vested with the authority of the state to keep law and order. Criminals and other outlaws will run riot over the city if the policemen do not enforce the law. Christ has given us the authority, we are to represent God and enforce the authority and victory He has already won on our behalf. Through spiritual warfare and prayer we can enforce this victory.

The Seed of Prayer

Even for those who have received no cure after prayer, the seed for healing has been sown. Something always happens when we pray for each other. It may not be in the form of an immediate physical or emotional cure, but always something happens, a stream of God's healing power begins to flow.

Sometimes healing comes in a most unexpected way and area, and not necessarily in the way we think it will. We should pray for healing or a miracle, but we never know how that miracle or healing will manifest itself. Sometimes healing is instantaneous, sometimes slow, sometimes the sick can feel themselves getting better and at other times they can't feel a thing. When we pray for healing it's like the parable of the mustard seed, it takes time but then gradually it begins to manifest; the stalk, the head and then the full corn. In the healing ministry the first step is to plant the seed through prayer. Sometimes some people get worse instead of better, but this need not shake our faith, when a seed is planted it dies before it begins to grow. We must not focus on symptoms but on God the Healer. It is tempting to give up nurturing the seed, but it is when we cannot see what is happening with our eyes that the most important work is being done. The authentic healing ministry for the most part is gentle, simple and quiet, not full of hype and theatrics.

The Progress of Healing

Healing is the restoration of diseased tissue, while a miracle is a creative action of the Spirit of God in man's life. God has designed the human body to heal, i.e. to be restored to health from disease or injury (through immune cells, platelets, growth factors which cause cells to replicate and bring about repair of injured cells or tissues), our prayers and faith can hasten this healing process. John G. Lake in his sermons 'adventures in faith' tells of observing the progress of healing in their 'healing rooms'. Within the building where the healing rooms where located, an X-ray outfit was incorporated where pictures of some healing prospects were taken. Among those pictured included a man with tuberculosis. Each time he was ministered to in prayer an x-ray picture would be taken. John G. Lake reports that as the pictures were taken you could see the progress of the healing. Each picture showed less and less of the disease until there was no more evidence of it and he was completely healed. John G. Lakes notes that; when you pray, something is happening to you. It is not a myth; it is an action of God. The power and life of God, that nature or essence of God, flows through your nerves, down through your person into every cell of your being and every square inch of your skin comes alive with the life of God. Prayer is God's divine dynamo. When you pray, the power of God comes into your heart, and it flows from your hands and into the souls of men, and God Almighty moves on their behalf. Sin dissolves; disease flees when the power of God approaches. When God comes into your life, your heart will not be satisfied with an empty Pentecost, but the light of God will flood your life. It is not our long prayers, says John Lake, but believing God that gets the answer. However sometimes persistence is needful. Paul says, of the powers of darkness we are praying against. "For we wrestle not against flesh and blood, but against principalities, against powers, against the rulers of darkness of this world against spiritual wickedness in high places (Eph. 6:12)". The word wrestle straightaway implies persistent struggle, exertion of strength and energy (in the spirit). Sometimes we have to lay hold of God, and stay before Him, through the darkest night until we breakthrough and the work is done. There is a prayer in the spirit, where the spirit of man and the Spirit of God unite and become one, we must stay in prayer until the Spirit has a chance to work out the problem[102].

Those who have considerable experience in the healing ministry have noticed that when prayer for healing is offered few are totally healed while some people experience some real improvement. When more time is spent praying for these people more improvement occurs, these gradual healings should not discourage us but are a sign of hope. When we see the sick our thoughts should be "if only someone could pray with that man or that woman in the wheel chair for several hours I believe he could walk". We have a wonderful ability to transmit the life of Jesus to people around us.

How to Pray for Healing

There is no one method or technique that produces results; God wants us to depend on Him and not on a technique. However there are some simple steps that flow out of the very nature of prayer for healing.

- We must first repent of all sin and forsake it, Jesus has not promised to destroy the works of the devil in our body while we are clinging to the works of the devil in our souls. It is hard to exercise faith for healing while cherishing or holding unto sin in our hearts (Ps 66:18, 1John 3:21, James 5:16). Departure from evil will bring health to our bodies Prov 3:7-8.

- We must totally surrender and submit ourselves to God; (Lev 8:10-12, James 5:14) the anointing with oil in the name of the Lord was an act of dedication and consecration implying a full surrender and submission (James 4:7).

- We must pray the prayer of faith and depend on the Holy Spirit to direct our prayer because He knows precisely how we should pray for a particular case.

- We must remember that symptoms do not always disappear instantly. Healing or recovery is sometimes gradual (John 4:50-52). The bible differentiates between miracles and healing (Mark 6:1-6). Many people miss healing by trying to confine God to miracles. Christ's promise is that "they shall recover" (Mark 16:18) but he does not say 'instantly'. "Faith means that we are confident of what we hope for, convinced of what we do not see" (Heb 11;1 Moffatt). Faith is not believing without evidence, it is believing because of the highest possible evidence; God's word.

- We must believe we receive when we pray.

- You may also break bread to re-enact the covenant by partaking of the broken body and shed blood of Jesus (1Cor 11:23-26).

- Obey any specific instructions from God impressed upon your heart e.g. God may instruct you to sow a seed towards your healing (money or otherwise), or carry out some form of restitution. Get rid of any occult material and repent of any involvement in occult practices this may include astrology, tarot cards, fortune telling, palm reading etc.

- Resist sickness just as you will resist sin – someone once said 'Let us put our sickness away by faith, as we would put away sin'.
- We must praise God for the answer Ps 50:14-15 even before you see the results, praise brings powerful deliverance (I am a living testimony).
- See yourself healed. Imagine yourself healthy and doing what you could not previously do. If you can see it, you can have it.
- Finally trust God totally, relax (this may be difficult if you are in pain) let go, and let God.

When we wholeheartedly believe and receive what God declares in His written word about the matter, then the Holy Spirit gives us the personal experience of Christ as our Physician.

Talking about physicians, we shall now examine what the medical profession has to say about the power of faith and prayer with respect to the healing and health of the body.

Chapter 13

Evidence From Medical Research
Is prayer good medicine?

Dr Howard Somervell (a fellow of the royal College of surgeons and a member of the Mount Everest Expedition in the early nineties) tells the story of a man with cancer of the cheek. The disease was so advanced that he declined to operate upon him. He was sent home to die. Then the patient remembered the power of God through prayer, and went to his local church and persuaded his fellow church members to have frequent and united prayer that his cancer may be cured. Some months later when the doctor went to the branch hospital near to his place of abode, a stalwart, healthy man with a healed scar on his cheek came to see him. The cancer, incurable by any method known to medical science (at least at the time), except radium and X-rays, had completely disappeared. The doctor was amazed because he was certain of the original diagnosis, there was no doubt about it. The

Doctor said "Explain these cases how you like, by the power of mind over the body, or by the intervention of God – the fact remains that their faith had been exercised in a way of which in our materialistic England we have no experience"[103].

When cancer slides its chilling fingers over the body of someone you love, arguments over whether or not to pray cease to be important – you pray. And perhaps you should. In this chapter we will examine what the medical professionals and researchers have to say about the effects of prayer, faith or religious activity on health and healing?

The dictum of the British Medical Journal reads "there is no tissue of the human body wholly removed from the influence of the spirit"[104].

Starting in the late 1980s a series of review articles began appearing in scientific journals that kept tabs on the growing evidence supporting religion's effects on health and mortality. The studies suggested a therapeutic effect of prayer. The evidence, though sometimes conflicting and over interpreted is nevertheless convincing

Many of the clinical studies carried out support the hypothesis that prayer plays some role in physical healing. The basic concept for the use of prayer in these studies was to see if adding prayer to standard high-tech treatment, could actually make people better, heal faster, get out of the hospital faster, make them need fewer pills and suffer less. The early result obtained from these studies were very suggestive that there may be a benefit to these 'prayer' therapies[105].

A significant body of research backs up the notion that personal prayer can be a healthful activity, if only because of the placebo effect. Remote intercessory prayer, on behalf of patients who don't know they are being prayed for, is quite another matter because the benefits from what may merely be psychic self-delusion are missing, and prayer has to speak for itself. The landmark study that began generating new interest was conducted by Randolph Byrd in 1984 and published in

1988. Byrd's objective was to evaluate the effects of intercessory prayer (IP) on patients admitted to a coronary unit. The study was conducted on 393 patients. Half of the patients received Intercessory Prayer (IP) from born-again Christians who prayed for them by first name away from the hospital. Byrd discovered that people in the IP group ended up with fewer patients suffering complications. The benefit of this study was that it used classic methodology for intervention evaluation and avoided many of the design problems found in earlier studies. Byrd's study was also unique in that the prayer offered was directed specifically to the Christian God[106].

In 1999 William Harris a cardiologist and several colleagues published a study similar to Byrd's in the archives of internal medicine. The Harris study involved 990 patients admitted to a coronary care unit. Once again patients were randomly assigned without their knowledge to a treatment or control group with the treatment group being prayed for by a team of outside intercessors. The study found that the treatment group registered better outcomes on a specially devised coronary-health scale. Harris concluded that this result suggests that prayer may be an effective adjunct to standard medical care[107].

Doctors attest to healing through prayer

In his book "The healing power of faith" Dr. Koenig defines healing as cure, recovery but also "the confidence to fight the illness" and faith he says is "the confident belief in a supreme being, which most people call God". "Faith gives people a tangible sense of mastery in their lives". Using both anecdotal and research data, he demonstrates that there is ample evidence to show that people who regularly attend church, pray, read and put in practice what the bible or their faith teaches are overall healthier. Just for starters they have significantly lower blood pressure, are hospitalised less, recover from surgery faster, have stronger immune systems and are likely to live longer. Their emotional health also benefits; family life is better and depression is lower. The research raises many questions e.g. are the health benefits caused by the life style and general belief of these religious groups?

Dr Koenig found that elderly people who were likely to rely on religious faith and prayer when under stress were much more likely to report little or no fear about death, when compared with their peers for whom faith and prayer were less important.

Harold Koenig, M. D. the director of Duke University centre for Religion/Spirituality and Health, together with his colleagues produced these groundbreaking findings:

- People who regularly attend church, pray individually, and read the Bible have significantly lower diastolic blood pressure than the less religious. Those with the lowest blood pressure both attend church and pray or study the Bible often.
- People who attend church regularly are hospitalised much less often than people who never or rarely participate in religious services.
- People with strong religious faith are less likely to suffer depression from stressful life events, and if they do, they are more likely to recover from depression than those who are less religious.
- The deeper a person's religious faith, the less likely he or she is to be crippled by depression during hospitalisation for physical illness.
- Elderly people with a deep, personal (intrinsic) religious faith have a stronger sense of well-being and life satisfaction than their less religious peers.
- People with strong faith who suffer from physical illness have significantly better health outcomes than less religious people.
- People who attend religious services regularly have stronger immune systems than their less religious counterparts.

- Religious people live longer. A growing body of research shows that religious people are both physically healthier into later life and live longer than their nonreligious counterparts. Religious faith appears to protect the elderly from cardiovascular disease and cancer.

Hundreds of major studies by other researchers have produced similar findings. For example religious hip-fracture patients recover faster than their non religious counterparts. After open-heart surgery, patients who find comfort in their religious faith are three times more likely to survive than nonreligious patients. The risk of dying from all causes is up to 35 percent lower for people who attend religious services once or more a week than those who attend less frequently[108].

In 1993, the privately funded National Institute for Healthcare Research (NIHR) in Rockville, Maryland, assembled hundreds of studies on the health benefits of religious faith and activity into a research guide called "The Faith Factor". The NIHR found that 77 percent of studies on the health benefits of religion demonstrate a positive effect, including in the areas of drug and alcohol abuse, emotional illness, chronic pain, cardiovascular disease and general health. Perhaps most interesting, religious faith was shown to increase people's overall survival rates. The social support which improves mental/emotional health enhances physical health. Also positive health habits of religious people play a great part in their general well being. Nevertheless, there can be no doubt that answers to prayer or divine intervention as a result of prayer plays a crucial part in the health of believers. Dr Koenig in his book gives the account of dozens of "medical miracles" he has seen in his practice. Concluding Dr Koenig states that it takes both a deep personal faith in God and active involvement in a faith community for people to obtain maximum health benefits. He notes also that there is now scientific evidence suggesting that the "content" of faith can make a difference in its healing consequences[109].

Another physician Reginald Cherry M.D. states that the medical field is now learning that a person's positive attitude in fighting and refusing to accept illness can literally change white blood cell count in the body, it can actually activate a defence the body naturally has against disease, and against cancer in particular[110].

When prayer has been put to test in actual experiments in hospitals, clinics, and laboratories, distant prayer does have an effect – in humans and non-humans, even when the recipient of the prayer is unaware the prayer is being offered. In May 1995 the Journal of the American Medical Association published an article titled "Should Physicians Prescribe Prayer for Health?" This article described the steadily increasing evidence that religious practice, including prayer, correlates with improved physical health. If the evidence favouring prayer is valid, as many experts believe, are physicians (or Christians) justified in ignoring it? In the face of an impressive body of scientific studies supporting prayer, holding back prayer from patients may be equivalent to deliberately withholding a potent drug or surgical procedure. Prayer is now a medical and scientific issue.

Today over 130 controlled scientific studies investigating the effects of intercessory prayer have been carried out and about two thirds of these show statistical evidence that prayer has a significant effect. In addition 250 studies show that on average, religious practice that includes prayer promotes health. A survey done by the National Institute for Healthcare research in Rockville, Maryland, found that 43 percent of American physicians pray for their patients[111].

Experiments with people showed that prayer positively affected high blood pressure, wounds, heart attacks, headaches, and anxiety. Other subjects in these studies included enzymes, bacteria, fungi, yeast, red blood cells, cancer cells, seeds, plants, mice, chicks etc. The processes that were influenced were the activity of enzymes, the growth rates of white blood cells, mutation rates of bacteria, germination and growth rates of various seeds, healing rates of wounds, size of tumours, rates of haemolysis of red blood cells and haemoglobin levels. The traditions of scientific research requires going through scientific data and not around it, no matter how uncomfortable or unconventional. A true scientist cannot ignore the evidence for prayer's effectiveness without feeling like a traitor to the scientific tradition. The evidence is simply overwhelming that prayer functions at a distance or close range to change physical processes in a variety of organisms, from bacteria to humans. These data are so impressive that they are regarded by some doctors as among the best-kept secrets in medical science. The results of some of these studies were so dramatic that a Doctor commented that if what was being tested was not prayer but a modern drug, this would have been heralded as a wonderful medical breakthrough and people would have lined up around the block to get their hands on it.

Studies with a variety of medical treatments have conclusively affirmed that the administering physician or researcher is not independent of the results[112]. If a doctor's beliefs can actually influence the action of medications, as these double-blind studies indicate, then this phenomenon may apply to prayer. Those who believe it works tend to experience more results.

Researchers have also looked at lower life forms because such organisms do not have a personal set of beliefs that could affect the outcome of the study. Bacteria as far as we know, don't do theology. In one study, researchers placed bacteria in test tubes and then divided the samples into 2 groups. They asked people some miles away to pray for one group that they would grow faster, in 14 out of 15 trials it worked. Researchers believe similar results occur when people are the objects of the prayer. When asked why healing prayer does not work all the time Larry Dossey MD states "nothing works all the time in medicine. When we use penicillin for strep throat, it fails 40%

of the time. When it doesn't work we don't blame penicillin (or stop using penicillin) why blame prayer because it isn't 100% effective? Why erect a double standard in which we demand more of prayer than we do of drugs and surgery (both of which do not work all the time). The miracle is that prayer works at all. No therapy is 100% effective, points out Dossey, because of our limited medical knowledge"[113]. Perhaps we do not get a hundred percent result in prayer due to lack of spiritual knowledge or limited understanding of the way God works.

The advocates of faith healing such as Benson state that the effect of prayer operates along certain biochemical pathways in the body. He states that praying affects epinephrine and other corticosteroid messengers or "stress hormones" leading to lower blood pressure, more relaxed heart rate and respiration. Recent research demonstrates that these stress hormones also have a direct impact on the body's immunological defences against disease. Also decades of research show that there is a healing power in faith. If a patient truly believes a therapy is useful even if it is a sugar pill the power of that belief has the power to heal. In one classic 1950 study, for instance pregnant women suffering from severe morning sickness were given syrup of ipecac, which induces vomiting and told it was a powerful cure for nausea. Amazingly, the women ceased vomiting. "Most of the history of medicine is the history of the placebo effect, comments Benson in his book; "Timeless healing". He also notes that his patient's progress and recoveries often seemed to hinge upon their spirit and will to live. He showed that repetitive prayer slows a person's heart and breathing rate, lowers blood pressure, and even calms brain waves, all without drugs[114].

Faith in the medical treatment (Benson writes) is wonderfully therapeutic, successful in treating 60-90% of the most common medical problems. But if you have believe or faith in an invincible and infallible force this carries even more healing power. So does that mean that the faithful actually have God on their side? Are their prayers answered? Benson doesn't say. But a true scientist, cannot dismiss this possibility says another doctor. It cannot be directly studied, but an honest scholar cannot rule it out. Science may never be able to pin down the benefit of prayer or spirituality, attempts by Benson and others to do so have been described as "trying to nail jelly to the wall". However others like Larry Dossey author of "healing words" says "we often know something works before we know why" (or how), therefore it may not be necessary to understand how prayer works to put it to use for patients[115].

The relationship between religion and health, on average and at population level, is overwhelmingly positive. The spiritual lives of human beings have something to say about their physical, mental and emotional well-being[116]. It is an irony that scientists are discovering persuasive evidence for the power of prayer at the very time when some theologians are calling into question the value of the ancient Christian tradition of praying for healing.

The Use of Medicine

How should we view medicines or medical intervention? Certainly we may use medicine if available and needed because God has created substances in the earth that can be made into medicine with healing properties. God sometimes heals directly through prayer; at other times through nature assisted by doctors who have learnt how the body can be assisted to throw off sickness that oppresses it. Medicines thus should be considered part of the whole creation that God considered "very good" (Gen 1:31). To refuse to use effective medicine insisting that God perform a miracle of healing instead of healing through medicine must be strongly discouraged by Christians. Of course our faith must not be in doctors or medicines instead of God, a mistake tragically made by king Asa (2Ch 16:12-13). But if medicine is used in connection with prayer, then we should expect God to bless and often multiply the effectiveness of medicine (1Tim 5:23). Even when Isaiah had received from the Lord a promise of healing for king Hezekiah, he still asked the king's servant to bring a cake of figs and apply it (as a medical remedy) to Hezekiah's boil (2 Kings 20:7). However, sometimes there is no appropriate medicine available, or medicine does not work. Certainly we must remember that God can heal where doctors and medicines cannot heal (and it may amaze us to realise how frequently doctors cannot heal, even in the most medically advanced countries). Moreover, there may be many times when an illness is not putting us or others in immediate danger and we decide to ask God to heal our sickness without the use of medicine, simply because we wish to exercise our faith and give him glory, and perhaps because we wish to avoid spending the time and money to use medical means, or we wish to avoid the side effects associated with some medicines. However a decision not to use medicines in these cases should be a matter of personal choice and should not be forced on others. We see Jesus healing in cases where medical means have failed, the woman with the flow of blood for 12 years could not be healed by any one (Lk 8:43-44) but was healed by her faith in Jesus. There is no doubt that a lot of people beyond the help of physicians who came whenever Jesus was teaching and healing were healed of their various diseases (Lk 4:40). A mistake sometimes made by Christians is to fail to see God at work in the natural as well as in the supernatural, through physicians and nurses as well as the prayers of believers. While it is true that the ministry of spiritual healing abounds, this does not deny all possibility of natural means or the role of the doctor. Ministry in the gifts or healing through prayer, while truly a blessing of God, does not negate medicine[117].

While the use of medicine has its benefits we must realise that many drugs may have an immediately soothing effect but they are not really a cure, they do not bring healing hence they are a form of disease management; they are at best a poor substitute for the wholeness and peace that comes from God. Some life saving drugs exist e.g. antibiotics which eradicates the micro-organism causing the illness but generally most drugs address the symptoms but not the root cause of disease.

Research can neither prove nor disprove the reality of answered prayer or divine intervention. To be sure, prayer does not need science to legitimise or justify it. However, if science can demonstrate the potency of prayer, people who practice and believe in prayer are likely to feel empowered and validated in their beliefs as a result. Scientific research into prayer is not bringing God into the laboratory to test Him; it is bringing the laboratory to God and opening a window to watch Him at work. Science and medicine is an important means through which God's healing power is channelled into our world. Nevertheless, the doctor can set the bone, cut out the tissue, or administer the drug but only the mysterious life force of God itself can join cells back together, restore chemical balance and reinstate health.

Chapter 14

Why Some Are Not Healed
What are the hindrances to healing?

The thorny question of why prayer for healing doesn't always seem to work is one that has baffled theologians and Christians for centuries. Why are some healed and others not healed? This is the 'million dollar' question and there is no shortage of theories. The inability to forgive, bitterness, lack of faith, is often cited as obstacles to healing. Some in the healing ministry say it is a question that cannot be answered.

From the instances of healing recounted in the Gospels and Acts we observe that there is evidently no limitation to the kinds of sickness from which people were healed. The sick, whatever their infirmities, were healed, this is true of Jesus (Matt 4:23), the totality of healing is significant. As a result of the coming of the Spirit, healing is now available to all. The statement "they were all healed" is a striking testimony to what the Holy Spirit can do through one like Peter who was an open channel and willing instrument. It remains a testimony to this day that the power of God to heal is still present wherever His Spirit abounds. Even as salvation and the forgiveness of sins is available to all, so also is the healing of all forms of physical ailments. There needs only to be, as in New Testament times, persons filled with God's Spirit, those who not only proclaim the gospel of new life in Christ but also minister healing in Jesus' name. However, as we have observed, not all in Acts were healed in every situation, also not all during Jesus' ministry, on one occasion when Jesus came to his own home town, he could only heal a few sick folk. It is clear that healing was restricted by the lack of receptivity and the unbelief of his town folk (Mk 6:3, 5-6). On another occasion at the sheep gate pool where there where a multitude of invalids (John 5:3), he only healed one. An atmosphere of unbelief many not have been the case here, it was Jesus' own decision to help the one on whom He took special pity. However it must be said that if any of the multitude of lame, sick and invalids had taken the initiative to ask Jesus for healing it is near impossible to imagine that they would not have obtained the healing for which they requested. Based on the record in the gospels and Acts, we may say that healing, while intended or available for everyone, may not be received by all. Such factors as a lack of receptivity or unbelief may be operative on the human side; all are not healed because not all will do all they need to do or know what they must do to obtain healing. However it must be said without reservation that the power of God's Spirit makes possible the healing of every kind of disease.

So why are some not healed?

There are so many possible reasons or combination of reasons why some do not receive the cure they desire. At times the reasons are obvious or revealed to us. In such cases removal of the obstacle will result in the cure. In other cases we do not know where the blockage is and so cannot remove it. If we could discover why people are not healed in every situation then the obstacle could be removed and healing would be achieved all the time.

However when healing does not occur what is to be our response? Are we to be stoic Calvinists and say this must be God's will so we must grit our teeth and bear whatever pain is dished on our plate? Or are we to re-modify our theology and say that God, no longer deals with us in such a manner and that healing is now out of divine fashion? Or do we insist that someone did not have enough faith? There are no easy answers for why some people are or are not healed. Are the worthy receiving merited favour? Or are a few being singled out for unmerited favour?

Medical research itself reflects the agony of failure, but medical research keeps on searching inspite of failure and keeps on overcoming hurdles. The continuing presence of sickness in this world is a sign not that God is uncaring, weak or absent but that we human beings have failed to be channels of God's healing power. Still failure is not something that should be feared as those who have no hope for restoration and renewal but to those who see God as a loving parent who wants our healing, our responsibility is to keep searching and working to overcome the blockages. If God is struggling to channel us power to heal, we can work to remove the obstacles in our lives, so that God's can be released to act. Healing prayer is risky because it requires us to let go of control and let God reshape us in the divine image. God's power to heal bodies shatters our prejudice that healing prayer is for the more emotional, less intelligent folks; that the bible stories of healing are merely "symbolic" and "not really true" and that the way the world is, is God's will. These prejudices are stumbling blocks to the fullness of God's kingdom on earth. The kingdom of God means liberation from the powers of death and freedom from the powers that squelch life.

An excellent analogy of healing prayer is given by A. Sanford[118], she says; when Thomas Edison had tried some hundreds of times to find a wire that could transmit a continuous flow of electricity, and had failed some hundreds of times, he did not say "it is not the will of electricity to shine continuously in my wire, instead he tried again. He believed that it was in the will i.e. in the nature of electricity to produce this steady light. He concluded, therefore, that there was some adjustment to the law of electricity that had not yet been made and he determined to make the adjustment. For more than 6000 times he tried again. And he succeeded in making electricity to shine continuously in a wire; that is faith. For Christians, faith does not simply believe that God exists, that is a fact. Rather, Christian faith believes that God is good and ultimately powerful, and acting accordingly, even when events are going badly. That is the faith, which led Jesus to the cross, and to resurrection.

Similarly, if our prayer for healing does not work, we must re-examine and reset our procedure yet another time, and try again. It is childish to blame God for every misfortune; we must begin to take responsibility for our part in the co-operative venture of healing through prayer. In this interim age, when the kingdom has been inaugurated in Jesus Christ but not yet fulfilled in the resurrected body for us all, we will experience shortcoming from time to time in our prayers for healing. But God's success increases as we study, practice and persevere with all the tools of our faith; from the bible and our experience, to the written reflection and experience of others. We ought to go to God and ask. Prov 25:2 says "It is the glory of God to conceal a thing: but the honor of kings is to search out a matter."

We might never fully understand the mystery of why some are not healed because it is not fully revealed to us. Throughout this book we have hinted at reasons why some are not healed but in this section we have put it all together and will briefly discuss the ones that have been plainly revealed to us in Scripture and through the experience of many.

Lack of compassion

When there is an absence of love, healing cannot occur. God is a God of compassion and to the degree that we can enter into His compassion for the sick and hurting is the degree to which we can be a vessel through which His healing virtue will flow. When we begin to develop true compassion for the sick and hurting God will begin to use us more in the Healing ministry of the Holy Spirit. Our faith for healing must be fuelled by love not self gratification or self glory. There are many examples of people who have been healed in a climate of love even without direct prayer.

Lack of knowledge

God uses many methods to heal, if you stick to one that He is not using you will not get results. If as a channel of healing to others you are unable to discern how God wants to heal, then healing may not come. Prayer is one way of co-operating with God to bring health to men. Medicine, surgery, good nutrition etc. are ways that we might receive our healing. We must find the way which is relevant to the case concerned. Jesus healed the sick in many different ways. Lack of knowledge is therefore a hindrance to healing (Hosea 4:6).

Unbelief

It is already well established in Scripture that faith in Christ produces healing while a lack of it will have the opposite effect. Unbelief blocks the healing power of God. Even in Jesus' home town unbelief limited Christ in what He could do to heal his own town folk (Mark 6:4-6). Faith comes by hearing God's word and when there is no teaching about healing or

God's willingness to heal, people will have no faith or confidence to ask or pray for healing. James 1:7-8 says a double man is unstable in all his ways he will not receive anything from God.

Sin

The root of all sickness is sin in one form or the other, either the original sin (Adam's sin), generational sin or personal sin (Isaiah 59:1-2, Exodus 20:5, Deut 5:9). Sin is well established as a hindrance to prayer and healing. Jesus commands some of those he healed to go and sin no more lest a worse thing comes upon them. God is first interested in our sanctification as a prelude to healing and deliverance. God does not answer prayer on a superficial level; He is interested in dealing with the root of the problem. He would be an unfaithful father if He let us keep our sins and blessed us anyway. (However, there is evidence from scripture and real life that God healed and delivered people who were not holy. In this His sovereignty must be acknowledged Rom 9:15). The sin of pride (Isaiah 57:15, James 4:6) disobedience, breaking the covenant is directly related to sickness and disease (Deut 28:59-61). Habitual or unrepentant sin can also block healing. Generational sin is a reason why some are not healed. 1Cor 7:14 says children are sanctified by believing parents, when parents repent of past sin and/or generational sins healing can be received by children.

Whatever the disease you are facing today, God can heal it including genetically inherited ones. If God created a gene perfect from the beginning of time and the devil, because of generations of sin and rebellion of man was able to alter the amino acid sequence which makes up the DNA, then God can restore it to its perfect form. If the devil has the power to mess it up, how much more can God's power restore it to wholeness. The devil is not more powerful than God. If the devil has messed up your family genes, then God can fix it! If the root of a disease is genetic then ask God to change the genes for you, have the faith of a little child, be daring, be audacious, it doesn't make any difference, asking for a change of genes or asking for bread, just ask! Healing of all disease is possible if God's conditions are met for spiritual healing. Prov 26:2 says the curse without a cause shall not come. When the cause or reason is removed the curse has no right to remain. The devil has no right to afflict us just because he wants to. If the devil could do as he wanted he would have eliminated all believers through disease, but the fact that he has not shows that he does not have the right to. God's protective covering is in place over us even as in the time of Job. The devil can only come in through an open door, historically, generational or personally, when we shut this door of sin, the hindrance is removed. Forgiveness of sins is intimately connected with bodily and emotional healing (James 5:15-16). Much physical sickness is a direct sign that all is not well between us and God or our neighbour.

Unforgiveness

Unforgiveness is a clear hindrance to healing. The Scriptures state clearly that forgiveness will be withheld from those who withhold forgiveness from others (Matt 6:14-15). When our sins are not forgiven by God we cannot hope to receive healing from Him either. Often forgiveness comes before healing. In Ps103:1-3 we see that the iniquities are forgiven then all the diseases are healed. Many people have some form of unforgiveness in their hearts towards one person or the other and this is a hindrance to healing.

Lack of Spiritual Discernment

When Jesus healed the sick, he did so in a variety of ways. Most of the time he healed by a word or touch. There were times when he healed diseases by addressing the spirit behind the disease or the spirit of infirmity e.g. Luke 13:11-12. Often times it is necessary to deal with the spirit behind a physical disease before healing comes and this has to be discerned by the help of the Holy Spirit. Some diseases are physical but others have a directly controlling spirit which must be cast out first in order to bring about healing. When dealing with cases that are not purely physical in origin it is helpful to obtain a history of the person to discover the possible open doors for sickness either inherited or personal. Many diseases are caused by spiritual issues which need to be addressed before healing can occur. Past or present involvement with the occult, dabbling into witchcraft and similar things can present a blockage to healing. Identifying and shutting those doors will deal with the root cause of the disease. Spiritual roots or blocks exist in many cases.

Divine mysteries & timing

There are some things in life which will always be unanswerable because we know in part and see through a glass darkly. In the story of the paralytic, John 5:1-15, Jesus took the initiative in the healing, the man did not seek for Jesus. The man had been in that situation for many years but it was on this day that Jesus chose to bring healing to the man. There is sometimes a divine timing with healing for reasons we will never know, in such cases healing will be realized in God's time.

Despising or not honouring the prophet

In Mark 6:3-6 we see that the people from Jesus' home town held up their own healing by dishonouring their Prophet. As a result Jesus could not do many mighty works among them. Miriam was afflicted with leprosy and her healing delayed 7 days because she spoke against Moses, the anointed leader (Num12:1-15). Dishonouring or speaking against anointed ministers of God (1Chr 16:22, Ps 105:15), murmuring complaining and ingratitude also block healing.

The sovereign will of God

If someone does not recover from prayer it may be that we cannot cooperate fully enough to help restore health because we do not know enough or have enough faith, love or knowledge or maybe some obstacles are blocking the flow of God's power. On some occasions, God may use illness for a purpose that we don't understand. On other occasions, God may intervene directly and still on other occasions, God may work indirectly through others. While we recognise the doctrine of divine sovereignty, this should no more prevent our asking in faith for the healing of our bodies than the doctrine of election should prevent our asking with fullest assurance for the salvation of our souls.

Expecting God to heal on our own terms

In 2Kings 5:8-14 Naaman had his own idea of how he wanted the prophet to heal him and he would have been included in the statistics of those who were not healed if not for the better judgement of his servant. He expected God to heal him in a dramatic or flamboyant way but Elisha simply said 'go wash in that dirty river and you will be healed' (paraphrased), he felt demeaned by the manner of healing suggested, he had lost his focus which was to be healed. He almost missed out on his healing because the method of healing offered to him did not conform to his own expectation. This attitude particularly looking for a loud miracle when God wishes a quiet or gradual healing may hinder some from receiving their healing. God never responds to man's demands to prove Himself, God acts on His own terms.

Neglect of natural means of preserving health

There are some natural and medical means through which God may bring healing or help us maintain health, failure to use these or a neglect of God's principles of healthy living (e.g. healthy eating, rest etc.) may also hinder healing. Unless we take ordinary care of ourselves, we cannot expect to be cured of our sickness through extraordinary means, we need to learn to keep our lives in balance[119].

Some do not really want to be healed

Believe it or not, some who have been ill for a long time do not actually want to be healed. They may have become comfortable with their situation and do not want to loose the pity, attention and assistance that come with their condition. When Jesus asked the paralytic in John 5 "do you want to be healed" his answer was "I have not a man". Some nurse and prefer their sickness because of the support and sympathy they get in that state. It is whatsoever we desire when we pray that the bible says we receive, so where there is no honest desire, no healing can be expected. The consecrated Christian will not consciously tolerate sin for a moment, and yet how tolerant some are toward sickness. They will even pet and indulge their sickness, instead of resisting them as the works of the devil.

Trusting man rather than God

When we begin to look to a man instead of God for healing, this itself can be a block to healing. God is the Healer, people are only channels, so our trust must be in God as our Healer (Jeremiah 17:5, 7, 9-10 2 Chron. 16:7-12). In the same way, the minister of healing must look to God and not to his own abilities or gifting. He must also be free of the need to prove a point; he must be free of any personal desire for achieving results for his own self image or ego. Healing is totally in

God's control and not within the control of man, this inability to control keeps us humble; it helps us realise where healing comes from.

Robbing God of tithes and offerings

Not honouring God with one's finances and withholding one's tithes and offerings from God opens people up to the devourer and to the curse and in some cases may hinder their healing (Malachi 3:8-11).

Not Praying Specifically

Praying in general terms howbeit eloquently will produce no results. We must ask specifically for what we desire and then leave it to God to decide how and when He will answer, but we must ask specifically. To pray a general prayer like "God bless this sick person" is not a very effective kind of prayer in most cases. A physician is of no help if he cannot specifically diagnose the problem. In the same way if we are not specific in our prayer we do not get much results. Even if we do not know all the details of the case we would be more effective in prayer if we are able to discern the nature of the problem; i.e. physical, spiritual or emotional.

Fear

Fear opens people up to all kinds of evil, particularly ill health. Fear is a negative emotion that can have detrimental effects on health and well-being. When you are in fear you are not in faith and without faith it is impossible to please God. When you are full of fear you are saying that God is not 'big' enough for your situation or your sickness is too big for God. The spirit of fear must be cast out before healing can be obtained. Meditating on 2 Timothy 1:7 is an antidote to fear. "Fear Not" is a command quoted in the bible some 365 times. It is a command that has rich benefits. Some people are so uptight, anxious and fearful that they hinder their own healing. Letting go and letting God take control may be the key that brings healing for some.

Giving Up

Jesus said in Luke 18 men always ought to pray and not to give up. Sometimes a fighting spirit is required to receive the healing we desire. Many give up before their break through. In Isaiah 38:1-5 when Hezekiah heard the prophecy from Isaiah that God had said he would die he did not shrug his shoulders and say que sera sera, he defied that contrary prophecy and cried out in prayer to God. God granted him healing and many more years. Too many people give up at the first sign of a hurdle but the truth is that victory often comes to the importunate.

Rejecting healing as part of the covenant today

This is a major block to healing that affects large segments of the church today. Because of the preaching that healing has passed away or that sickness is God's gift most do not have the faith for their healing, though they seek healing contrary to the doctrine they embrace. It is a statistical fact that those who do not believe that healing is part of the covenant available today often do not experience divine healing. Faith for healing comes by hearing the word continually preached about God's willingness to heal today. Some people believe falsely that sickness is God's will, but the truth is if you see a person depressed and burdened under the weight of disease you may be reasonably sure that his sickness is not God's gift at all. But if he believes that God has sent this sickness then he is very unlikely to receive his healing.

Inability to be totally yielded to God as His instrument of healing

I think one of the key reasons why some are not healed through our prayer or ministry is because we are not totally yielded and tuned to the Spirit as we should be. We have not become the precision instruments needed by God; able to channel God's healing power without hindrance. In ophthalmology there is a precision instrument which is a 0.12mm toothed forceps; it is used in cataract operations. These forceps must grasp tissue half a mm. thick and hold it firmly enough to pass a needle through it while exacting no pressure to the open eye. If the instrument is not grasping properly the consequences are dire. We must become like this 0.12mm forceps, grasping with finely tuned and perfectly aligned hearts whatever God wants us to grasp. We must be exactly what He wants us to be holding the sick so the Great Physician can bind up and heal. Jesus was able to heal all who came to him for healing because he was God's precision instrument per excellence. He did exactly what He saw the Father do, he could not do anything unless he saw the father do it, he was one with the father always (John 5:19, 10:30). Hence God's healing power could work and move through Him without hindrance. He knew or was able to discern the root of disease and the precise method by which each sickness was to be healed. Some ministers have indeed been like a precision instrument in God's hand and have been greatly used of God[120]. How we desperately need to be totally yielded to God that He may be able to use us as His precision instruments for healing.

Despite these obstacles to healing, faith leaves us no doubts about God's power and desire to heal. Though we must also acknowledge that we do not know all the circumstances required to pray rightly for every person. Sometimes we are partially in the dark when it comes to praying for healing, consequently we can never say for sure that everybody we pray with will receive healing, since we know in part and see in part. Unless the Lord reveals all the necessary details of a situation we simply do not know it all. But does this mean we lack faith? No, I don't think so; it simply means we are human; my faith is in God not in my own ability – not even in my own faith.

Not everybody receives the healing they seek: This is a mystery hidden from men. But I believe that God heals and that His ordinary will is that everyone be healed.

Chapter 15

The Final Verdict
Is God's will always healing?

Mr GD developed a serious heart condition diagnosed by his cardiologist as a myocardial infarction (malfunction of a valve which allowed the blood to flow between two ventricles of his heart). He experienced several heart attacks and almost died. The cardiologist decided to regulate the heartbeat by inserting a pacemaker in his chest in the hollow below the collarbone during surgery. A tube extended over his lung down into his heart. A small battery in the pacemaker provided an electrical charge which sent steady impulses into his heart, keeping the beat regular. Eight months after the surgery Mr GD visited his father in Donora, Pennsylvania. His father who was an usher at the Kathryn Kuhlman miracle services invited him to come along. Mr GD was reluctant, he was not a very religious man but his father prevailed upon him. At the close of the service Miss Kuhlman came down the isle, praying for people, when she got to Mr GD she laid hands on his head and moved on, Mr GD fell "under the power" and felt a terrific burning in his heart similar to one he had felt during his first attack. The pain finally subsided and he was able to crawl back to his chair, he felt spiritually renewed. Later in the evening after his bath he stood before a mirror drying himself and noticed that the scar from the surgery to insert the pacemaker had vanished. The next morning he re-examined himself and the scar was still no where to be found. Hesitantly he went to see his doctor after some weeks. When the cardiologist checked his cardiogram, it was perfect but when Mr GD explained what happened in the meeting he attended, the doctor reacted with anger. He called for an examination and the pacemaker could not be found, the doctor accused Mr GD of taking it out. Mystified, he replied "if there was a scar made to put it in, wouldn't there be a scar if someone took it out"? Then he added "yes God took it out, and removed the scar also". The doctor was enraged. The following week, Mr GD kept an appointment at the hospital where he was examined by a panel of cardiologists, including a professor of medicine from Harvard. All agreed it was the most unusual case they had ever witnessed. Dr. George Johnston, of Philadelphia, another consulting physician during Mr GD's earlier heart attack, was willing to testify (the attending cardiologist said he did not want to be made a laughing stock of the medical profession, so he refused to testify). Dr. Johnston however states "I can confirm that Mr GD had a heart attack, that a pacemaker was placed in his body, and that now the pacemaker and the five-inch incision scar are gone. It's all in the record"[121].

Has healing passed away with the apostolic age?

Some say that divine healings or miracles can't happen today, they ended with the apostles. Others say that they won't happen today; they served their purpose and were withdrawn. Yet, others say they don't happen today; they faded out and are seen no more. But the view in this book is that they can happen today, they do happen today and will happen where the required conditions are fulfilled. This is the position that is faithful to the evidence. Surely if divine miracles simply did not happen today and have not happened since New Testament times, it leaves many answers to prayer utterly inexplicable. What about all the alleged miracles in various Christian groups and at different times between the apostolic times and now, are they all to be dismissed as make believe? Surely the theory that says miracles or supernatural gifts of healing ceased with the apostles is clearly wrong. Time or space will not permit all the evidence to be presented in detail but enough has been said to settle it for anyone who is not wedded to a divergent theory, that from the first days of the Christian church right on through the centuries until today there have been miracles, healing and the manifestation of the gifts of healing.

Does God desire perfect health for his children?

From what we see in Scriptures it is right to ask God for healing. Jesus tells us to pray "Deliver us from evil" (Matt 6:13). James said (5:14) "...Is any amongst you sick let him call for the elders and let them pray..." If it is right to ask God for healing then it must be right to expect God to grant healing. Moreover, Jesus healed all who were brought to him, he never sent people away, telling them it would be good for them to remain ill for a longer time. Even the syrophoneacian woman obtained healing for her daughter through her persistent faith, though it appeared that Jesus did not wish to grant healing because she was a Gentile and not from Israel. (Jesus' mission was to the house of Israel and not to the Gentiles at that time).

Whenever we take any kind of medicine or seek medical help for an illness, by those actions we admit that we think it to be God's will that we should be well. If we thought that God wanted us to continue in our illness, we would never seek medical means for healing! So when we pray it seems right that our first assumption (unless we have specific reason to think otherwise) should be that God would be pleased to heal the person we are praying for. As far as we can tell from Scripture, this is God's revealed will. It can be assumed that if we want to understand God's attitude towards healing we should look at Jesus' life and ministry. If Jesus reveals the character of God to us, then we can stop speculating and arguing over God's will in sickness and healing. Jesus healed people because he loved them. Very simply, he had compassion for them; he was on their side, he wanted to help them[122]. This is a strong argument, especially when coupled with the realisation that Jesus came to inaugurate the presence of the kingdom of God among us and to show us what the kingdom of God would be like. How then should we pray, certainly it is right to ask God for healing, and we should go to Him with the simple request and quiet confidence that He would give physical healing in time of need. Those in the church who do not pray for healing for fear of disappointment need to know that this is not the right attitude or solution. Telling people that God seldom heals is not beneficial to faith. People need to be told that God heals today and is willing to heal them in whatever way He chooses.

Nature itself shows God's attitude towards the healing of the body. The body is designed by God to heal itself. As soon as disease or germs enter our bodies, the body begins to expel them. Break a bone, or cut a finger, and your body will do its utmost to heal, and usually succeeds. This self healing activity of the body reveals God's will. If sickness is God's will then it would be a sin to desire or seek to get healed and every doctor, nurse or medical personnel would be violating God's will. The natural instinct of every sick or afflicted one is to find relief or restoration to health. This instinct is in line with God's will. If God wants some of His people to remain sick for His glory, then Jesus, during His earthly ministry robbed God of all the glory by healing all who came to Him. If sickness is sometimes given to make us obedient and more saintly why do we all do our best to rid ourselves of sickness? So does God not chasten us through sickness? He certainly does, when we disobey. Sickness may be allowed, through the Father's loving discipline, but God has told us just how it may be avoided and prevented (1Cor 11:31-32). By self judgment we avoid chastening or punishment. Divine healing is not unconditionally promised to all regardless of their conduct (Exodus15:26).

In Luke 12:16 Jesus attributes sickness to the work of the devil "Ought not this woman whom Satan hath bound, lo, these 18 years, be loosed from this bond.."? Jesus Christ was saying; the lawful thing, the proper and appropriate thing is for this woman who has been bound all these years to be loosed. By healing the sick Jesus was doing His Father's will, i.e. destroying the works of the devil (1John 3:8). Many today would have said to the woman who had been sick for 18 years, accept your sickness it is the Lord's will. God is trying to teach you something. But Jesus asks a rhetorical question; "ought not this woman.... whom Satan has bound this many years be loosed?" We should be asking the same questions today.

For those who say God wants some to remain in sickness or that God gives sickness to make them more holy and that the sick should bear sickness patiently, can they seriously say these words to a demon possessed person. It would be monstrous and unthinkable. So why would anyone say God's will might be for the sick to remain sick, when both demon possession and physical sickness are all one and the same; one the sickness in the mind, the other of the body.

Jesus taught us to pray "thy will be done on earth as it is in heaven" This very prayer shows that it is not God's will which is prevailing on earth today; it is largely the devil's will in the form of sickness disease, wars, famine, disasters etc. Since God's will is health, when disease and sickness come upon us, he will again and again act as our Healer. Thus we should not hesitate to move boldly in the area of gifts of the Spirit or prayer of faith or whatever means might be needed to bring healing to us and others who need it. Gifts of healings, gift of faith, working of miracles, prayer and faith have been permanently placed in the church (1Cor 12:28). To the degree we are open to such gifts, desire such gifts, and minister such gifts, God will be glorified and his people richly blessed. The living Lord Jesus through the Holy Spirit is ever ready to bring healing[123].

Is healing for all?

The greatest barrier to faith for healing today is the uncertainty in our minds whether it is God's will to heal all. It is impossible to boldly claim by faith a blessing that we are not sure God offers to all, because the power of God can be claimed only where the will of God is known. Faith begins where the will of God is known. If it is God's will to heal only some of those who need healing, then none have any basis for faith, unless they have a special revelation that they are among the favoured ones. Faith must rest on the will of God alone, not on our desires or wishes. The only instance in the ministry of Jesus when someone came to Jesus with doubts about his will to heal was the case of the leper Matt 8:2, "Lord if thou wilt, thou canst make me clean" the first thing Jesus did was to correct his theology "I will; be thou clean" (v.3). Someone said "if healing is for all we will never die" (what a daft thing to say). This is absurd because God never planned that people should die through sickness, his will is that they die in peace (Ps 104:29) when they have fulfilled the number of their days (Exo 23:25-26). God promised to take sickness and disease away from His people but He did not promise that they would never die when their time was up.

To say that the promise in Exo15:26 is not for God's people today is to change God's "I **am** Jehovah-Rapha" to "I **was** Jehovah-Rapha". He is the same yesterday, and today, and for ever" (Heb 13:8). Why would God withdraw this Old Testament mercy of healing from the new covenant and dispensation which is better than the old? Let the sick go through the gospels and note that no man ever appealed in vain to Jesus for healing. Matt 4:23-25, Matt 9:35-36, 12:15, 14:14,34-36, Luke 6:17-19. If according to modern tradition, it is God's will for the sick to patiently bear sickness for his glory, is it not strange that there should not be even one of this type of person in all these multitudes who were brought to Christ for healing? By healing the epileptic boy that the disciples could not heal (Mk 9:14-29), Jesus proved that it was the Father's will to heal even when his disciples (who had done many mighty works) failed to heal the boy. Jesus by healing him showed them that the failure to heal proved nothing but unbelief or lack of prayer power. Is it not possible that some of those not healed today who feel that this is God's will fall into this category? The command in James 5:13-18 is to "any sick" in the church, not to a select few who have been able to discern if it is the will of God to heal them. Also He states that the prayer of faith will heal the sick, thus we can interpret this to mean - any sick one in the church can be healed by the prayer of faith. God would not command "any sick one" to call for prayer if it were no His will to heal them in the first place. In Ps 105:37 we observe that healing was available to all "...there was not one feeble person among their tribes..", and in Num 21:8 everyone that was bitten, when he looked upon the bronze serpent (a type of Christ) lived.

Why God heals

There are many reasons why Jesus healed the sick and understanding some of them will help us understand why it is certain that healing continues today and that God desires perfect health for all his children.

Compassion - Jesus healed because he had compassion (Ps 145:8-9 Matt 14:14, Mark 1:41). Faith rises mountain high when the truth of God's present love and compassion dawns upon the minds and hearts of the people. It is not what God can do that inspires faith; it is what God wants to do or yearns to do that inspires faith. It is not faith in God's power that secures His blessings, but faith in His love and in His will. The Lord is gracious means he has a disposition to show favours. It does not take much faith to believe that God is able but not many truly believe that God is willing. The willingness of God actually means it gives Him delight to be merciful to us (Mic 7:18). God is looking to and fro for opportunities to gratify His benevolent heart 2Chron 16:9. Judges 10:10-16 gives us a glimpse of the compassionate heart of God. The Israelites had been disobedient to God; pursuing Baals and forsaking the God of their fathers. When they began to suffer oppression as a result of their idolatry, they remembered God and began to seek Him. God's response to their prayer was that they should go and get help from the Baals to which they had been devoted (v. 14). The Israelites continued to plead with God and He finally conceded. Verse 16 says God helped them because 'he could no longer bear to see Israel suffer' (NRSV), the amplified version says God was 'impatient with the misery' of his people, the KJV says 'His soul was grieved for the misery of his people' and the NKJV says his soul 'could not endure the misery of his people'. When we suffer through sickness, God cares, He is deeply touched, and feels for us. Psalm 103:17, 13, 11 says "The mercy of the Lord is from everlasting to everlasting upon them that fear him" (v.17) "Like as a father pitieth his children, so the Lord pitieth them that fear him"(v.13), "as the heaven is high above the earth, so great is his mercy toward them that fear him" (v.11). Compassion moved the Lord to heal the leper " ....And Jesus moved with compassion, put forth his hand, and touched him,... and saith unto him, I will; be thou clean..."(Mark 1:40-42, 45), compassion moved him to heal the multitudes "....and saw a great multitude, and was moved with compassion towards them, and he healed their sick (Matt 14:13-14). Out of compassion he healed two blind men who cried for mercy (Matt 20:29-30, 32-34). Christ healed because he had compassion when he saw the needs and suffering of the sick in his day. Are the needs of sufferers today different from the time of Jesus? And do they not need as much compassion as anyone ever did in the past? Could the loving Son of God, who had compassion upon the sick, and healed all who came to Him for healing, cease to be touched by the sufferings of his own after He had become exalted at the right hand of the father? Has He ceased to be merciful, has His compassion failed? (Lamentations 3:22-23, Ps 103:17). I don't think so; it is the church that has changed. If God healed in the first century because of compassion why would He be content to demonstrate that compassion today only by giving grace to endure the suffering rather than grace to heal the condition? If God has power to help but doesn't, I don't know what it means to say to a sick person "God loves you". The idea of God's love and goodness can be deeply shaken when we deny that he heals today. If God does not ordinarily answer prayer but wants us to accept and endure suffering, what then is the Good News?

Healing is a foretaste of complete redemption - The Holy Spirit and His work in us is "the earnest" (foretaste) or guarantee of our inheritance until the redemption of the purchased possession" Eph 1:14. The earnest or guarantee of a glorious body is the immortal life of Christ touching our mortal bodies (and bringing healing to it) with a foretaste of redemption. When we experience healing the life of Jesus is made manifest in our mortal flesh (2Cor 4:11).

Healing is a mighty evangelistic tool - Christ and his disciples drew the multitude with miracles. Miracles and healings do not divert people from the more important matter of salvation of the soul, rather it encourages it, more people will get converted as a result of miracles or healing they have seen or experienced than without it. Healing could be rightly called one of the greatest evangelistic tools of our day. Although the greatest miracle is new life, a new birth wrought by the word is not immediately visible. Hence when a visible sign accompanies the word, there is undeniable attestation to the reality of what has been inwardly wrought by the message of salvation. The world will be more attracted to a healthy church than a sick one.

For his glory - Jesus said "When he, the Spirit of truth, is come.... He shall glorify me" (John 16:13-14). How will the Spirit glorify Christ if men cannot do the greater works or works of power that Jesus promised before he ascended? (John 14:12-13). How could the Spirit glorify Christ without continuing the healing ministry of Christ through the church? How can the Holy Spirit the Healer, the miracle worker arrive and then miracles and healings be withdrawn?

Demonstration of the Power of God - The value of the ministry of healing is not in the mere fact that people are healed. The value of healing is more largely in the fact that it becomes a demonstration of the living inner vital power of God, which should dwell in every believer and make us new and mighty men in the hands of God. When we are baptised of the Holy Spirit we are equipped with the power of God to be a blessing which includes being a channel of God's healing power. We need God's power to meet the demands of this age.

From the reasons given we observe that God heals because He wants to glorify himself and His son. He heals because He has deep compassion for the suffering. He heals in response to our faith and in response to His own promise and command to the church (James 5:14-16). God also heals to teach us about Himself, or simply because we asked and for sovereign purposes known only to Himself. None of these reasons are based on the changing circumstances of the first-century church. They are rooted in the nature and character of God and His eternal purposes. The ministry of healing stands at the centre of the Christian faith. Christ not only expected his 12 disciples to be healers. Later He sent the 72 evangelists with the specific mandate to preach repentance and to heal the sick (Mk 6:12-31, Lk 9:1-6). Today he expects it of us, generations later. He expects us to be channels through which His healing waters will flow, so that everyone to which these water shall come, shall be healed.

Ezekiel 47:9

> And it shall come to pass, that every thing that liveth, which moveth, whithersoever the rivers shall come, shall live and there shall be a very great multitude of fish, because these waters shall come thither: for they shall be healed; and every thing shall live whither the river cometh.

The Mystery of Healing

On this side of heaven there are some things about healing that will remain a mystery. Some who God has used powerfully in the healing ministry and have championed the cause of divine healing have ended up dying of sickness or disease. We don't understand why this is the case, but what we do know is that we need to be extremely careful when used as channels of God's power. We must be careful to give the enemy no room in our lives. We must be humble and careful not to speak against those who have fallen. Our God is a consuming fire He will not share His glory with man.

In the arena of healing we must be careful not to expand any one method or experience into a universal method. We must pray to God in faith and confidence; but we do not tell God when or how to do it. God teaches us over and over again that He is beyond our limitations and will not be boxed into our neat little compartments.

Chapter 16

Practical Suggestions
For Healthy Living
How can we maintain good health?

Sophie (not her real name) was about eight years old, and had always been a sickly child, suffering from various types of infection at one point or another. Someone suggested she start drinking goat's milk and almost immediately her health improved dramatically. Another 3 year old girl whom I will call Lily always had a runny nose, cold, cough and ear infection, her parents read a study that said that two thirds of infants have some allergy to cow's milk, so they switched her to goat's milk and within two days she was totally cured.

Diet
After some study, observation and a bit of experimenting, I

have come to the conclusion that – what you absorb into your body must affect how it functions, what you eat cannot help but contribute to how you are. "You are what you eat" – is fundamentally a true statement. Food provides your cells with the nutrients that serve as their building blocks and protect your cell's important functions like energy production and immunity. Food is the source of nourishment and energy to support the health of our body. Research shows that eating a healthy diet can help prevent or reduce the severity of various diseases. E.g. asthma, cancer, diabetes, osteoporosis, irritable bowel syndrome, Chrohn's disease, migraine etc. Poor nutrition directly leads to degenerative disease and poor health.

The flip side to this statement is that good nutrition can lead to a longer healthier life. Your physical well being is to a very large extent dependent upon what goes through your mouth. Regardless of your genetic make up what you consume day after day is what is assimilated through your digestive system and becomes part of your physical body. If you eat healthy food or junk food it will go in and become integrated into your flesh, literally you become what you eat.

In order to understand the impact of our diet on our health it might help to view your bodies as a machine or a car which requires fuel to function optimally. The right kind of fuel ensures the smooth running of our cars but the wrong type of fuel will clog up the system and eventually cause it to break down. Naturally our bodies are so much better designed than the best of machines and so we can go for decades on a poor diet but eventually it will begin to show signs of distress.

In considering a healthy diet, I like to keep in mind two key factors; assimilation and elimination. Aim for wholesome foods that provide good nourishment and essential nutrients to be assimilated into your body. Endeavour to eat nourishing foods which aid efficient elimination of by-products of digestion. Nourishing foods are wholegrain products, fish, eggs, milk, sweet potatoes etc, such foods contain essential nutrients and micronutrients. Foods which aid bowel movement, elimination of waste and potentially harmful by-products of digestion such as free radicals include foods rich in fibre and antioxidants e.g. fruits, vegetables, unrefined wholemeal foods etc. and water (water is absolutely essential). The following list of foods have been described as healing foods by some top nutritionists; fish and fish oil, barley and wheat, cow or goat milk (Proverbs 27:27), olive oil, grapes, figs and berries, soups/stocks, healthy saturated fats e.g. extra virgin coconut oil, honey (Proverbs 24;13, 25:16, 27), free range meats, seeds, eggs, green leafy vegetables, organ meats[124].

The food we eat usually has an almost immediate impact on our health. For instance children who have an allergy to cow's milk could benefit greatly by changing to goat milk. Goat milk is by no means a panacea for all childhood illness but it must be said that it has made a great difference to the health of some children. Goat milk is also more easily digested and is said to be closer to human milk than cow's milk. Infants under one year however should be breast fed or given formula milk as their main milk. Goat milk does have its drawbacks; it is low in folic acid and Vitamin B12.

Exodus 23:25 says "I will bless your bread and water i.e. your food and will take sickness away from you. Deut 7:11-15 talks about God blessing our corn, oil and wine and taking sickness away from us. Looking at these scriptures I get the impression that our health is linked to our food and that one of the ways that God keeps us healthy is by blessing our food and making it nourishment to our body. However I don't think He will bless junk food if that is what we eat continually. Food is meant to be enjoyed but there are other reasons why we eat. Food is fuel, nourishment and for preservation of health. The body uses the nutrients in our food to grow, heal and repair itself, to maintain good health and proper functioning of the cells tissues and organs. So when next you eat you might want to bear this in mind and ask yourself "can God bless this and can my body use this to keep me in optimum health".

Exercise

The bible says physical exercise profits little, forget about the 'little', and let's concentrate on the 'profit' bit. No matter how little at least there is some profit. Brisk walking is one of the most effective, easiest, most accessible forms of exercise. It can be time saving too because it can be easily incorporated into any lifestyle and it will not cost a penny in gym or club membership. Swimming is also a very good form of exercise.

Rest

Rest is absolutely necessary for good health. Rest is crucial to the health of the body and soul. If you don't want to burn out or get stressed out, my advice is take a break every 7 days i.e. 1 out of every seven days. I believe that is how God designed it. God created the earth in six days (whether literally or not) and he rested on the seventh. I don't believe He needed a rest because He was tired. He created a day of rest to illustrate a principle, and I think we should take that seriously. Our bodies have been created so wonderfully by God that a lot of time we subject it to abuse or inadequate rest for so long yet it still continues to perform but it may not do so forever if we continue to mistreat it and disregard the instruction manual of the Maker. There is simply no substitute for quality sleep. Sleep is so vital to health that it has been referred to as the most important non-nutrient you can get[125].

Laughter, fun happiness

Laughter they say is good medicine, Proverbs 17:22 states that a merry heart doeth good like a medicine...", research has shown this to be true. There are anecdotal accounts of people who were treated using laughter 'therapy'. They had been suffering from psychological problems and depression, then they were given humorous videos, comedies and the like to watch for hours on end. They laughed and laughed and they became healed. These were basically psychological illnesses and not physical, but because some sicknesses are psychosomatic (Mind/body) in nature when the soul/mind is healthy, a healthy body usually follows. Research into the physical benefits of happiness proved conclusively that "laughter, happiness and joy are perfect antidotes for stress. It is said that the diaphragm, thorax, abdomen, heart, lungs and even the liver are given a massage during a hearty laugh"[126]. Scientists have discovered that everyone develops cancerous cells in their body weekly. But certain cells of the immune system cells called 'natural killer (NK) cells' are specifically designed to attack and destroy abnormal cells. I studied medical immunology at Masters level, and I know that fear, worry, stress and other negative emotion actually weaken the immune system and these 'natural killer cells'. Therefore if we go through life anxious and stressed out constantly, we weaken our immune system and make ourselves susceptible to sickness and disease. The reverse is also true. A joyful and cheerful heart is healing to the body. Laughter can strengthen the immune system and increase production of immune cells. So let your hair down, rejoice in the Lord and have some fun.

Forgiveness/ love

Many stories abound about people with one sort of chronic disease or the other who found no cure until they give forgiveness and released long time hurts and offences. Being angry and vengeful is detrimental to our health. "Be angry, but sin not, do not let the sun go down on your anger", so says Eph 4:26. As much as lies within your power, live peaceably with all men (Rom 12:18 paraphrased), this is a biblical health warning. We know from scripture that unforgivess hinders our prayers, so forgiveness could be the key to recovery and healing for many long term illnesses. The bible makes it clear that we cannot obtain forgiveness for our sins if we don't forgive others. Living under this kind of judgement is sufficient on its own to bring illness.

Prayer/communion

Studies have shown that those who pray, read their bible, sing and attend church are less likely to complain of sickness, or visit the doctor. When I talk of prayer here I mean spending time in God's presence having fellowship with Him. Psalm 16:11 says 'In his presence there is fullness of joy, at his right hand are pleasures for ever more'. Spending quality time in prayer, praise and worship in God's presence no doubt has health benefits. Partaking of the bread and the cup also releases the life of God (1Cor 11:24-26, John 6:53-54). He is the Life giver, the Light, Healer and Restorer of His people. Moses beheld God and his face shone with God's glory. Time spent with God soaking up His presence and His divine life will bring restoration, renewal, refreshing and replenishment to you. A daily communion with our precious Saviour will cause us to know him as both sustainer of our spiritual life and natural health. And also our indwelling renewer. I have found this to be true in my experience. If you ever find yourself sick or you have a sick child, quieten your soul and sit in God's presence and worship Him from your heart, cast all your cares upon Him, relax and just worship Him. God inhabits the praises of His people, when we worship God He shows up. When He shows up, sickness cannot withstand His glory. Do this consistently and you will find that sickness cannot cling to you for long, disease dissolves and looses its hold in His presence.

Peaceful/Positive environment

I am a 'sucker' (pardon the expression) for a peaceful environment. I love peace so much I will do almost anything to maintain it. I just cannot function in an atmosphere of chaos, strife or heaviness. In my teens, there were times when home was not the best place to be. On a particular occasion after a Christmas holiday, things had been pretty stressful and as a result I became quite ill. I was at university at the time and had to return to the campus the following day. Despite my condition I went off to school. As soon as I left that negatively charged environment I got better immediately and within a day or two I was totally back in tip top condition. Never underestimate the effect that a negative environment has on health/stress levels. Many workers testify of poor health and stress as a result of a stressful work environment or unfriendly work colleagues and the same goes for stressful marriages and homes. High stress or unhappy negative environments can affect you psychologically and reduce your immune system's ability to fight disease adequately. When we are faced with danger or trouble the basic human instinct is the fight or flight reaction. This reaction causes a release of adrenalin (hormone produced by the adrenal gland and it converts stored sugar into glucose used for energy) needed for the fight or flight. The chemicals released when you are angry or stressed for prolonged periods have a potentially damaging effect on health. If the body is in a continuous state of fight or flight, the body equilibrium is disrupted and this can be potentially harmful to the body and may produce abnormalities in body function. These include the so-called psychosomatic disorders i.e. mind/body related disorders. The antidote to stress and anxiety is the peace of God, the bible says be anxious for nothing but in everything by prayer, supplication and thanksgiving make your request to God and the peace of God which passes all understanding will guard your heart and mind through Christ Jesus Phil. 4:6 (paraphrased). Peace and anxiety cannot mix; they are mutually exclusive i.e. to say the presence of one excludes the other. Hatred and bad relationships cause all kinds of sickness which usually remains until the root cause is removed. Much sickness is caused by wounded relationships, and restoration to harmonious relations is the solution.

Change your thinking and your words

Your thoughts deeply affect your health and entire well being. Proverbs 4:23 (NLT) says "Above all else, guard your heart, for it affects everything you do". Prov 23:7 says; as a man thinks so he is. There is a long list of diseases caused or exacerbated (made worse) by emotional stress. They include, glandular disorders, allergies immune system problems, infections, skin diseases, digestive, circulatory, genito-urinary, nervous, system disorders and even cancer[127].

Negative thoughts lead to negative words, when we speak negative words they affect us negatively because the words we speak out of our mouth affects our entire being. Your subconscious mind picks up your words, treats them as true, valid statements, then sets about trying to fulfil them. Your words create an atmosphere for good (healing) or evil (sickness), and you are going to have to live in that environment created by your words. There is a miracle in your mouth. If you want to change your world, start by changing your words. I talked extensively on the power of words in a previous book *"A Matter of Life & Death"*.

Faith and positive thinking, based on God's word, are vital keys to recovery or maintaining good health. Prov.17:22 refers to the connection between the soul and the body, medical science also attests to this mind/body connection. There is a gland called the hypothalamus gland referred to as the 'brain' of the endocrine system. This gland responds to thought and to the environment of your life and it plays an important role in many psychosomatic illnesses. In my imagination I see the hypothalamus gland as the link between your body and soul/ spirit or the connection between your thoughts and body. The hypothalamus acts as the body's watchman. It has sensors that detect changes in the blood. It is informed of emotions through tracts that connect it with the emotional centres of the brain. When a stress situation arises the hypothalamus is stimulated to react through various pathways of the body and produces alarm reactions. These alarm reactions produces increase in the levels of blood sugar and oxygen to organs that are most needed to ward off danger e.g. brain, skeletal muscles and heart. The point of the science lecture is this; fear, stress and anxiety affect our bodies negatively and until we deal with them our prayer for healing will not be effective. The solution to fear is salvation and deliverance freely offered by the Prince of Peace (Isaiah 9:6). When we continue in His word and walk in love we will experience perfect peace (John 14:27, 1John 4:18, Isaiah 26:3, Psalm 119:165).

Chapter 17

Your Daily Medicine
God's word

Dodi Osteen was healed of metastatic cancer of the liver, by the power of God's word[110]. She deposited God's word about healing in her heart and spoke it out of her mouth consistently and it defeated cancer. Its been more than twenty years since she was diagnosed with cancer and a few weeks to live, today she is alive and totally healed of cancer.

God's word is life unto those who find it. It is health and healing to all their flesh (Prov. 4:22). In the Hebrew, the word 'health' means medicine. Therefore what the verse is saying is that God's word is medicine to our body. If God's word is medicine, how do we take it? We take it by speaking it, by meditating on it and imbibing it. By allowing it to control our thinking until it becomes the stuff (fabric, cornerstone, composition) of our lives.

Life & death is in the power of the tongue. What we say continually out of our mouth affects our health and well being. Don't keep talking about how sick and tired you are, declare the health and strength that is yours in Christ. The bible says, let the weak say I am strong. You will be satisfied with the fruit of your mouth. The same way you feed your body with food, feed your soul/spirit with the word of God by speaking that word out of your mouth. Proverbs 18:20 says a man's innermost parts will be satisfied with the fruit of his mouth.

A story is told about a doctor who understood the power of words. He prescribed it to all his patients (in addition to their normal prescription). He told them to say at least once every hour "I am getting better and better every day, in every way". His patients experienced amazing results, compared to the patients treated by the other doctors.

Confession of God's word must begin before sickness comes, you don't begin to confess when you start seeing symptoms. You need to maintain a confession of good health, however if you are currently in ill health it is never too late to start now. Confession is not denying the facts, but proclaiming your desired end based on the word of God. God called things that were not, as though they were already manifest, in order that they might be so. You should do the same.

Below you will find some passages of Scripture (paraphrased), that you can speak daily into your life to help build your faith and to release the word of life concerning your health.[128]

I diligently hearken to the voice of the Lord my God, I do that which is good in his sight, I give ear to his commandments, I keep all his statutes and he will not allow any of the diseases of the Egyptians to come upon me, for he is the Lord my God that heals me. (Exodus 15:26)

I serve the Lord my God and he shall bless my bread and water and he takes sickness and disease far away from the midst of me. (Exodus 23:25)

I attend to God's word, I do not let it depart from my eyes, I keep it in the midst of my heart, for they are life unto me, and health and medicine to all of my flesh. (Prov 4:20-22)

Bless the Lord O my soul and all that is within me bless his holy name, bless the Lord o my soul and forget not his benefits, he forgives all my iniquities, he heals all my diseases, he redeems my life from destruction, he crowns me with loving kindness and tender mercies, he satisfies my mouth with good things so that my youth is renewed like the eagle's (Psalm 103: 1-5)

I am delivered from the curse of the law because Jesus hung on a tree for me; he became cursed for my sake. Sickness is a curse of the law therefore I am delivered from the curse of sickness and disease. (Gal 3:13)

Surely he has borne away my sickness and carried away my pains. He was wounded and pierced for my transgressions, he was bruised for my iniquities, the chastisement needful to obtain my wholeness and well being was laid upon him and by his stripes and bruise I am healed. (Isaiah 53:5)

He sent his word and healed me and delivered me from destruction. (Psalm 107:20)

The Spirit that raised Jesus from the dead dwells in me, that same Spirit quickens my mortal body. (Romans 8:11)

The Lord will restore health to me and heal me of my wounds. (Jeremiah 30:17)

Jesus came that I might have life, therefore I have life in all its abundance. (John 10:10)

A Personal Invitation to Wholeness

God created us for Himself and our hearts remain sick until we find Him. Peace with God is the first step to total healing. If you do not have a personal relationship with God, invite Jesus the Prince of Peace Jesus into your life today. You can pray this prayer for your physical and spiritual healing right now.

"I acknowledge that I am a sinner, desperately in need of your love and forgiveness. I believe in my heart that you sent your Son Jesus to die for my sins; he shed his blood for me on the cross and rose again from the dead. I invite Jesus into my life today to be my saviour, healer and deliverer. Thank you Jesus for saving me and making me whole (John 3:16, Rom 10:9-10).

We Want to Hear from You

My prayer is that you will experience healing and wholeness as you read this book. Please share your testimonies with us. If you need us to pray along with you for your healing you may send us your prayer requests.

To contact me, write to:

yomi@pneumasprings.co.uk

REFERENCES

1. Lewis, C.S. *A Grief Observed* 1969 by N.W. Clerk (New York: Seabury Press) pp.9-36 Quoted in MacNutt Francis Healing (Ave Maria Press, Notre Dame Indiana 1974)p100-103

2. Simpson, A. B. *The Gospel of Healing* (London: Morgan and Scott 1915,),15

3. Gordon, A.J. *The Ministry of Healing ;or Miracles of Cures in all ages* (London: Hodder & Stoughton, 1882),19

4. Wilkinson, John *"Physical healing and the atonement"* Evangelical Quarterly 63, (1991)149

5. Petts, D. *"Healing and the Atonement"* Dissertation Abstracts A2b (Ph.D. diss. University of Nottingham 1993),43-23

6. Baxter, Sidlow J. *Divine healing of the body*, (Zondervan: Grand Rapids 1979),125

7. Frost, Henry *Miraculous Healing*, (Marshal, Morgan and Scott London and Edinburgh, 1951),59

8. Gordon, A.J. *The Ministry of Healing ;or Miracles of Cures in all ages* (London: Hodder & Stoughton, 1882),26

9. Wilkinson, John *The Bible & Healing: A medical & Theological Commentary* (Grand Rapids: Eerdmans, 1998),270

10. Warfield, Benjamin B. *Counterfeit Miracles* (New York:1918, reprint, Edinburgh: Banner of Truth Trust1976),5.

11. MacNutt, Francis. *Healing* (Ave Maria Press, Notre Dame Indiana 1974 p131-132

12. Kelsey, M. *Healing & Christianity* pp. 7-11 Augsburg Fortress 1995

13. Ibid p. 11

14. MacNutt, Francis. *Healing* (Ave Maria Press, Notre Dame Indiana 1974) p64

15. *Luther's Works.* American Edition, 55 vols St. Louis: Concordia Publishing House Minneapolis: Fortress press 1955-86

16. Calvin, John *Institutes of Christian Religion* IV.18 (1953), 2:636 Translated by Henry Beveridge. Grand Rapids, MI: Wm.B. Eerdmans.,

17. Anderson, Sir Robert *The Silence of God.* Grand Rapids, MI: Kregel Publications, 1952 pp.153-54

18. Boggs, Wade *Faith Healing and the Christian Faith* Richmond, VA: John Knox Press, 1956.

19. Boggs, Wade *Bible and modern religions "Faith healing cults"* Interpretation 11.1 Jan 1957

20. kierkegaard, Soren. *Training in Christianity* 1944 pp.9-39 Translated by Walter Lowerie. Princeton, NJ: Princeton Uni. Press

21. Husserl, Edmund *Phenomenology and the Crisis of Philosophy,* Translated by Lauer pp.169-172 NY: Happer & Row, 1965.

22. Bultmann, Rudolf *Jesus Christ and Mythology,* p.15. New York: Charles Scribner's Sons, 1958

23. MacNutt Francis *Healing* (Ave Maria Press, Notre Dame Indiana 1974) p75 -86

24. Williams, Rodman J. *Renewal Theology Vol1:* Zondervan publishing House Grand Rapids, Michigan 1996 Pg 168

25. Grudem, Wayne *Systematic Theology* Inter-Varsity Press 1994 p369

26. Deere, Jack *Surprised by the Power of the Spirit* Zondervan publishing House Grand Rapids, Michigan 1993

27. Virkler, Henry *Principles and processes of Biblical Interpretation* Baker Books Grand Rapids, Michigan 1981 p.212

28. Fee, Gordon & Stuart Douglas *"How to Read the Bible for all its worth"* Scripture Union 1993 pp.106,108

29. Deere, Jack *Surprised by the Power of the Spirit* Zondervan publishing House Grand Rapids, Michigan 1993

30. Williams, Rodman J. *Renewal Theology Vol2:* (Zondervan publishing House Grand Rapids, Michigan 1996) 252

31. Wilkinson, John. *The Bible & Healing: A medical & Theological Commentary* Grand Rapids: Eerdmans 1998. P. 56

32. Baxter, Sidlow J. *Divine healing of the body,* Grand Rapids: Zondervan 1979. P56

33. Bosworth, F.F. *Christ the Healer* Whitaker House

34. Gordon, A.J. *The Ministry of Healing; or Miracles of Cures in all ages* (London: Hodder & Stoughton, 1882) pp.19-20

35. Baxter, Sidlow J. *Divine healing of the body,* Grand Rapids: Zondervan 1979. pp177-180

36. Gordon, A .J. *The Ministry of Healing or Miracles of Cures in all ages* (London: Hodder & Stoughton, 1882)p .226

37. Wilkinson, John. *The Bible & Healing: A medical & Theological Commentary* Grand Rapids: Eerdmans 1998. P65

38. Ibid. p141

39. Weatherhead, Leslie *Psychology, Religion and Healing* Hodder and Stoughton, 1951 p56

40. Kelsey, Morton *Healing & Christianity,* Augsburg Fortress 1995 p72

41. Ibid. p75-76

42. Wilkinson, John *The Bible & Healing: A medical & Theological Commentary* Grand Rapids: Eerdmans 1998 pp.148-152

43. Ibid. p156

44. Williams, Rodman J. *Renewal Theology Vol1:* (Zondervan publishing House Grand Rapids, Michigan 1996) 158

45. Wilkinson, John. *The Bible & Healing: A medical & Theological Commentary* Grand Rapids: Eerdmans 1998 p287

46. Gordon, A .J. *The Ministry of Healing or Miracles of Cures in all ages* (London: Hodder & Stoughton, 1882) p.218

47. Wilkinson, John. *The Bible & Healing: A medical & Theological Commentary* Grand Rapids: Eerdmans 1998 p287

48. Ibid. p173

49. Ibid. p191

50. Baxter, Sidlow J. *Divine healing of the body,* Grand Rapids: Zondervan 1979 p174

51. Wilkinson, John. *The Bible & Healing: A medical & Theological Commentary* Grand Rapids: Eerdmans 1998, p192.

52. Ibid. p193

53. Ibid. p193

54. Bosworth F.F. *Christ the Healer* Whitaker House pp.130-147

55. Frost, E. *Christian Healing: A Consideration of the Place of Spiritual Healing in the Church Today in the Light of the Doctrine and Practice of the Ante-Nicene Church* (London: A.R. Mowbray & Co. Ltd., 1940) p. 236

56. Wilkinson, John. *The Bible & Healing: A medical & Theological Commentary* Grand Rapids: Eerdmans 1998, pp.232-235.

57. Seckendorf, V.L. *Historical Commentary on Lutheranism and the Reformation* (Leipzig:1688-1629) Vol.3,p133. This account is quoted by Gordon, A.J. *The Ministry of Healing ;or Miracles of Cures in all ages* (London: Hodder & Stoughton, 1882) pp.111-112

58. Seckendorf, V.L. *Historical Commentary on Lutheranism and the Reformation* (Leipzig:1688-1629) Vol.3,p133. This account is quoted by Gordon, A.J. *The Ministry of Healing ;or Miracles of Cures in all ages* (London: Hodder & Stoughton, 1882) pp.111-112

59. Kelsey, M. T. *Healing & Christianity in Ancient Thought and Modern Times:* (SCM Press London 1973), p.233

60. Gordon, A. J. *The Ministry of Healing; or Miracles of Cures in all ages* (London: Hodder & Stoughton, 1882),p26

61. Warfield, Benjamin B. *Counterfiet Miracles* (New York:1918, reprint, Edinburgh: Banner of Truth Trust 1976)

62. Ibid pp.37-38

63. Deere, Jack *Surprised by the Power of the Spirit* Zondervan

publishing House Grand Rapids, Michigan 1993 pp.75, 273-274

64. Baxter Sidlow J. *Divine healing of the body*, (Grand Rapids: Zondervan, 1979), p.31

65. Ibid, p.31

66. Ibid, p.32

67. Ibid, p.33

68. Ibid, p.34

69. "*The letters of St.Ambrose*"No.22 pp.17-18 quoted in Weatherhead, Leslie. Psychology, Religion and Healing Hodder and Stoughton, 1951 p.86

70. Baxter Sidlow J. *Divine healing of the body*, (Grand Rapids: Zondervan, 1979), p.47

71. Ibid p.47

72. Ibid p.47

73. Ibid p.76

74. Ibid p.77

75. Ibid pp.80-86

76. Ibid p.87

77. MacNutt Francis *Healing* (Ave Maria Press, Notre Dame Indiana 1974)p58

78. Kelsey, M. T. *Healing & Christianity in Ancient Thought and Modern Times:* (SCM Press London 1973), p.234

79. Ibid, p.235

80. Garlick, P.L. *Man's Search for Health* (London: The Highway Press, 1952) pp.205-207

81. Weatherhead, Leslie. *Psychology, Religion and Healing* Hodder and Stoughton, 1951 p.89

82. Anderson, Sir Robert. *The Silence of God.* Grand Rapids, MI: Kregel Publications, 1952 pp.153-54

83. Baxter Sidlow J. *Divine healing of the body*, (Grand Rapids: Zondervan, 1979),62

84. Ibid. p46

85. Odulele Albert *"Testimonies of Almighty God"* OVMC publications 2004

86. Dutch Sheets *Intercessory Prayer* Regal Books California USA 1996 pg15-18

87. Baxter Sidlow J. *Divine healing of the body*, (Grand Rapids: Zondervan, 1979),p.200

88. Weatherhead, Leslie. *Psychology, Religion and Healing* Hodder and Stoughton, 1951, pp.238-239

89. Ibid. pp.239-240

90. Lake John G. *Sermons by John G. Lake*, His life, His Power 'Adventures in Faith' (Kenneth Copeland Publications) p465

91. Baxter Sidlow J. *Divine healing of the body*, (Grand Rapids: Zondervan, 1979),pp.212-227

92. Buckingham Jamie *"Daughter of Destiny"* Bridge Publishing Inc. New Jersey p.158

93. Dutch Sheets *Intercessory Prayer* Regal Books California USA 1996 p. 103

94. Ibid. p. 22

95. Weatherhead, Leslie. *Psychology, Religion and Healing* Hodder and Stoughton, 1951 p.93

96. MacNutt Francis *Healing* (Ave Maria Press, Notre Dame Indiana 1974)p277

97. Zodhiates, Spiros, ed. *The Hebrew Greek Key Word Study Bible* KJV Revised ed. AMG Publishers Chattanooga TN, 1991 p.1586-7

98. Lake John G. *Sermons by John G. Lake*, His life, His Power 'Adventures in Faith' (Kenneth Copeland Publication)

99. Zodhiates, Spiros, ed. *The Hebrew Greek Key Word Study Bible*

KJV Revised ed. AMG Publishers Chattanooga TN, 1991 p.1745

100. Dutch Sheets *Intercessory Prayer* Regal Books California USA 1996 p.97

101. Ibid. pp.203-211

102. Lake John G. *Sermons by John G. Lake,* His life, His Power 'Adventures in Faith' (Kenneth Copeland Publications)

103. Weatherhead, Leslie. *Psychology, Religion and Healing* Hodder and Stoughton, 1951, pp. 240-241

104. Quoted from Weatherhead, Leslie. *Psychology, Religion and Healing* Hodder and Stoughton, 1951, pp. 375-376

105. Davis, Jeanie *"Can Prayer Heal?"* The Saturday Evening Post Vol. 273 No.6 (Nov/Dec 2001) pp.14-16, 60, 64.

106. Thomas, Gary *"Doctors who pray"* Christianity Today Vol. 41 Jan 6 1997 pp 20-4

107. Cullen, Murphy *"Thy will be done"* Atlanta Monthly 1993 Vol.287 No.4 April 2001 p18-20

108. Koenig Harold M.D. *The healing power of faith* Touch Stone:Simon & Schuster New York 2001 p.24

109. Ibid. p.297

110. Osteen Dodi *"Healed of Cancer"* Lakewood church publication Houston Texas 2003

111. Dossey Larry M.D. *Prayer is good medicine* (Harper SanFrancisco 1996) p.p.65-71

112. Dossey Larry M.D. *Healing words* (Harper SanFrancisco 1993) p. 136

113. Bourne, Christine *"Prayer: It's just what the doctor ordered"* U.S. Catholic Vol.62 Oct 1997 p.25-30

114. Benson, Herbert M.D. *Timeless Healing* Fire Side: Simon & Schuster New York 1996

115. Wallis, Claudia *"Faith and Healing"* Times Vol. 147 June 24

1996 p.58-62

116. Koenig, McCullough & Larson, *Hand book of religion & Health* Oxford University Press 2001 p.

117. Grudem Wayne *Systematic Theology* Inter-Varsity Press 1994 p1064-1065

118. Sanford Agnes *The Healing Light* Published by Ballantine Books, a division of Random House New York

119. MacNutt Francis Healing (Ave Maria Press, Notre Dame Indiana 1974)p256-258

120. Buckingham Jamie *"Daughter of Destiny"* Bridge Publishing Inc. New Jersey pp.189-191

121. Ibid. p.181

122. Wayne Grudem *Systematic Theology* Inter-Varsity Press 1994 p1066

123. Williams, Rodman J. *Renewal Theology Vol2*: Zondervan publishing House Grand Rapids, Michigan 1996 Pg375

124. Jordan Rubin, S. *'The maker's Diet'* Published by Siloam Lake Mary Florida 2004 pp.145-154

125. Ibid. p. 55

126. Ibid. p. 165

127. Ibid. p. 161

128. Akinpelu Yomi, *A matter of life & death* Pneuma Springs Publishing 2003

SOME BOOKS BY PNEUMA SPRINGS PUBLISHING

A Matter of Life and Death
Yomi Akinpelu (£5.99)
ISBN 0954551001
This book is about the power of the words you speak and how you can harness that power to chart the course of your life to your destination.

A Basket of Flavours
Ode Andrew Eyeoyibo (£9.97)
ISBN 0954551028
This book contributes to the debate on the issue of moving the Church from Revival to Reformation.

Power to the People
Nancy Lazarus (£9.00)
ISBN 0954551036
This is about events and experiences of the ordinary man in an African nation, when the country's government changed from colonial rule to an independent country.

Cyber Evangelism
Esther Ogbonda (£6.99)
ISBN 0954551044
This book describes how we can use the internet for evangelism, and presents a variety of tools and approaches which have been used to spread the gospel over the centuries.

Sermons and Prayer
Rt. Rev (Dr) S L O Emmanuel (£5.99)
ISBN 095455101X
This a collection of the author's written and spoken thoughts over the years. Its practical application of the Word of God to everyday life makes the book relevant for this and every age.

It's the End of the World as we know it
Richard Bradbury (£9.99)
ISBN 0954551060
A user's guide that will enable you to grasp the end time prophecies in the Bible. It will help readers to understand end time events and decipher mysterious personalities such as the beast, the antichrist and the false prophet.

Mystery, Deceit & a School Inspector
Bryony Allen (£6.99)
ISBN 0954551095 (Fiction)
This book is set in a Primary School which has been subjected to a justifiably scathing Ofsted inspection. The death of one inspector rips apart the school and its inhabitants, wrapping them in mystery and deceit.

Working Wonders at Work
Ode Andrew Eyeoyibo (£6.99)
ISBN 0954551052
This book examines the attitudes to work and asserts a number of principles designed to make work an enjoyable experience.

The Creator's Diet
Nicola Burgher (£5.99)
ISBN 0954551087
"An insightful book. The Creator's Diet tackles some difficult biblical issues on food and diet and brings out a clear healthy eating message.

The Inevitable War
Norbert Seshie (£5.99)
ISBN 190580900X
This book reveals how the human mind is a battlefield and the inevitability of spiritual warfare, the devices and arsenals of the enemy, the weapons of our warfare and the recommended strategies for spiritual warfare.

Eden's Diamond
Damian Hono (£9.99)
ISBN 1905809018 (Fiction)
Eden's Diamond is a thrilling story with the themes of conspiracy, corruption and necrophilia; which combined, sets the stage for a bloody revolution in the most populous black nation on earth.

Yomi Akinpelu